British Population

WITHDRAWN

R. M. Williams
Sevenoaks School

HEINEMANN EDUCATIONAL BOOKS
LONDON

Heinemann Educational Books Ltd
48 Charles Street, London W1X 8AH
LONDON EDINBURGH MELBOURNE AUCKLAND
HONG KONG SINGAPORE KUALA LUMPUR NEW DELHI
IBADAN LUSAKA NAIROBI JOHANNESBURG
KINGSTON PORT OF SPAIN

British Library C.I.P. Data
Williams, Robert Michael
British Population – 2nd ed. – (Studies in the British Economy)
1. Great Britain – Population – History
301. 32′9′41   HB3583

ISBN 0 435 33960 5

Printed Offset Litho and bound in Great Britain by
Cox & Wyman Ltd, London, Fakenham and Reading

PREFACE TO THE SERIES

Most economics text books attempt to cover the subject within a single volume and in consequence some topics are treated briefly: often these same topics are those whose subject matter changes most rapidly. At present in order to keep up to date in the field of economics recourse must be made to a vast field of diffused literature including bank reviews, government publications, newspapers and various journals. With these problems in mind this series was conceived. The series consists of specialized books on those topics which are subject to frequent change or where the sources of information are too scattered to be readily available to the average student. It is intended that each book will be revised at frequent intervals in order to take account of new developments.

Derek Lee
General Editor

PREFACE TO THE SECOND EDITION

For this new edition the author has included more up-to-date statistics and used them in extensively revising the text to provide a better understanding of recent changes in population trends. The book opens with a general consideration of the importance of population studies in economics and a summary of early theories of population. The author goes on to look at the nature of pressure of population. He provides a summary history of British population and an analysis of its structure, migration patterns and possible future development. Finally he considers population policies in a British and a world context.

ACKNOWLEDGEMENTS

The author and publishers are grateful to the following for permission to reproduce copyright material on the pages indicated:
The Controller of Her Majesty's Stationery Office for the official statistics, on pages 34, 37, 40, 53, 58, 63, 81, 83, 89, 90, 91, 95, 96, 101; *Barclays Bank Review*, 116; *DEA Report*, 105, 107; *The Economist*, 89, 92, 94, 115, 116, 117; *The Guardian*, 86; *The Institute of Race Relations*, 65; *The National Institute Economic Review*, 73; *Oxfam*, 22; *United Nations*, 99.

CONTENTS

CHAPTER 1
THE IMPORTANCE OF POPULATION
AND EARLY POPULATION THEORIES

The importance of population

Professor Lionnel Robbins defined economics as 'the science which studies human behaviour as a relationship between ends and scarce means, which have alternative uses'. Scarcity is a product of aggregate demand outstripping aggregate supply of goods and services. Since men are born to play at least two economic roles in life – those of producer and consumer – population is at the centre of this human science.

In every economy there are four factors of production, two of which are human factors and two are not: land, labour, capital and entrepreneurship. The task of the entrepreneur is to combine land, labour and capital together so as to produce an increasing output of goods and services, which will satisfy the needs of the people living in the economy. These needs belong to the consumers within the economy, and when translated into money terms represent the demand for goods and services which the producers must work to satisfy. The human factors, labour and entrepreneurship, play a part in both the roles of producers and of consumers. So that 'with every mouth, God sends a pair of hands'.

The structure as well as the size of the population is important for the development of the economy. For instance, in developed economies, where child labour is forbidden and children stay on at school until aged 18–19 years, and may then go on to a course of further education, the burden of dependent children who are consumers, but not producers, is very great. And when men and women retire from producing in their early sixties, as they do in the United Kingdom, a further layer of dependants is added to those who consume but do not produce.

The size of the population is important for the development of the economy in other ways. For centuries man was bound by the needs of subsistence, and the ever-present fear of poverty and under-nourishment. He was caught up in the problem of producing sufficient food and clothing to provide a living for his wife and children, and as a result, seldom had time for anything other than the basic essentials. Later, much later, in economic history, as a result of specialization of labour, man's horizons broadened. With a larger population it became possible to specialize in the production of one good and buy in the other goods which were produced by other specialists. At this point man had moved from the subsistence economy to the exchange economy.

The importance of population is seen here not just to be providing sufficient specialists, but in providing a big enough market for there to be economies of large-scale production. This consideration is frequently advanced as the most pressing argument for Britain's entry into the European Economic Community. Alone Britain has a home market of 55 millions; as a member of the E.E.C. there would be a market of some 240 millions, appreciably larger than that of the United States, whose industrial pre-eminence has owed much to the existence of a large home market.

The study of population is called demography. The demographic unit is the family. It is almost universally accepted as the basic unit within human society. It is the most intimate of all group-relationships enjoyed by man. It is within this basic unit that the vast majority of demographic decisions are made. These decisions determine family size, and in the case of marriage, modify two families and create a new one.

Demographic statistics tell us a good deal about man in society. They tell us much about a society: its attitudes to average family size, the popular ages for marriage, the changing life expectancies, social and religious attitudes to moral problems such as illegitimacy, contraception, abortion and divorce. Wars, revolutions, medical epidemics, such as the plague of Medieval days or the influenza epidemics of this century, and even technological failures such as the New York blackout of 1965, when a power cut plunged the whole of New York into darkness for several hours, all find their way into demographic statistics because these events all have some demographic effect.

The study of population has assumed greater significance than ever in recent years. A century and a half ago, Malthus conjured up the spectre of overpopulation; now it is once again concerning the world's scientists, economists, and politicians. A glance at recent headlines in the national press, bring home to the reader the fact that a study of population is of prime importance to anyone trying to understand the nature of the world they live in. Nor is the problem

simply seen in terms of population growth outstripping food production. The social strains of large scale urbanization, environmental pollution, loss of rural amenities, and the increasing pressure
on both economic and human resources which follows rapid population
growth all cause increasing concern.

The Census

The most accurate recording of a country's demographic statistics
is the national census. In Britain a census has been carried out every
ten years since 1801, with the exception of the war year 1941. Because
the Census is used as a basic set of statistics for economic and social
planning programmes, great care is taken over its production. The
questions are becoming increasingly comprehensive (the 1971 Census
was the most complete yet attempted, with some 29 questions), and,
because of the increasing mobility of the United Kingdom population
and the need for more careful analysis, the practice began in 1966
of recording a mid-decade census on a small, 10% sample population.
Although a mini-census is open to sampling errors, it is hoped that
it will provide reasonably reliable guides to population growth and
changes in structure in sufficient detail to allow the modification of
social and economic policies.

The statistics provided by the census are used as a basis for a large
number of policy decisions covering areas of economic and social
planning. Like the National Income 'Bluebook', they are basic
statistics providing a solid foundation of knowledge on which policy
decisions can be taken by both central and local government. For
example, the leaflet explaining the importance of the Census, which
was handed to all households during the 1971 Census, listed under
the heading 'It's a big form with a big job to do' the following areas
of importance on which statistics were required for planning and
research to be carried out – housing, schools; industrial training,
medical schools and hospitals, transport, and key personal questions
such as the average age of marriage, the average number of children
or the work patterns of women with families and so on. The questions
asked by the Census were as follows:

1. How do you and your household occupy your accommodation?
   – owner occupied, rent from council, furnished letting, unfur-
   nished letting.
2. How many rooms are there in your house?
3. Is any part of your house shared with another household?
4. How many cars or vans are used by your household?

3

5. Has your household the use of the following amenities?
   - a cooker
   - a kitchen sink
   - a bath or shower
   - hot water supply
   - flush toilet (outside building)
   - flush toilet (inside)
6. Name of every person living in house
7. Date of birth of every person living in house
8. Sex of every person living in house
9. Relationship of each person to the head of the household
10. Marital status of each person living in house
11. Did the person have a job last week?
12. Is the person a full time or part time student?
13. Where was the person born?
    - in England and Wales
    - Scotland
    - Northern Ireland
    - other country – state year of entry to Britain
14. Country of birth of person's father/mother
15. Person's usual address a year ago
16. Person's usual address five years ago
17. Person's educational standards – A Level, HSC, ONC, OND
18. Educational experience since age of 18
    HNC, HND
    Nursing qualification
    teaching qualification
    degree or diploma
    graduate or corporate membership of professional institution
    any other vocational qualifications
19. Name and business of person's employer
20. What is the person's occupation?
21. Was person employee, self-employed, or an employer?
22. Is the person an apprentice in any way?
23. How many hours a week does he work?
24. Full address of the person's place of work?
25. Means of transport to work?
26. Was the person's employment a year ago the same as today?
27. Month and year of birth of each child born to person in marriage (to be answered by women)
28. Month and year of marriage (to be answered by women)

29. Month and year of divorce if person is divorced (to be answered by women)

It is worth considering what the value of each of these questions is in social and economic policy making.

How population changes: population projections

The most obvious change that occurs in a population is a change in its total size. This can take place either through natural increase or by a net immigrant inflow or a net emigrant outflow. Natural increase results from births exceeding deaths, either by an increase in birth rate (the number of births per thousand of population), or by a decrease in death rate (the number of deaths per thousand of population), or by a combination of the two. Net migrant flows occur when either more people leave the country than come in, making for a net emigrant outflow, or when more people come into a country than leave it, making for a net immigrant inflow.

Just as important as changes in the total population are changes in the composition of the population. Changes in sex distribution, age distribution, marital distribution, occupational distribution, regional and locational distribution, are vital for recording the changing macro-economic structure.[1]

One major purpose of demography is to forecast trends of population within the country. Care must be taken with population projections as the following extract makes clear:

It is of course impossible to predict with any confidence how large the population of Great Britain will be in a hundred or even in fifty years time. Population forecasts can always be upset by changes in fertility. But for some decades it is possible to make fairly confident estimates on the basis of existing trends; and hardly anyone believes that the birth rate, which has been falling rapidly in recent years, will rise in the near future, even if it does not fall still further. It is, to say the least, highly probable that in twenty years' time the population will not exceed 40,000,000.

This extract is taken from *The Common People* written by G. D. H. Cole and Raymond Postgate in 1938 when fear of a declining population held the thinking public, a fear that was given some official support in the Royal Commission on Population of 1949. Twenty years after the book was published, the total population of the

---

[1] For full explanation of terms, see glossary at the end of Chapter 1.

United Kingdom was 51·6 millions. It is important therefore to understand that all projections contain a great margin of error. The projections can be altered by a mass of inter-relating factors, which may be economic, social, political or technological.

The most recent official projections of the United Kingdom population were calculated by means of a complex computer formula.[1] The four elements of the calculations were:

    starting population
    mortality
    migration
    future births

Starting populations are important as they provide a base from which to begin research and projection. Care must be taken to plot the same base population right through – for instance the *de facto* or home population or the total population (See glossary p. 14). Mortality rates must be considered against a background of recent history. Death rates at different ages can then be calculated to give age-specific death rates, rather than crude death rates, for the former are a much more meaningful figure on which to base projections (see glossary). Migrant flows can be very difficult to project with any certainty because of their dependence on a wide range of factors not all of which are under the control of the home economy or government. However, assuming government immigration policy to remain unchanged, government departments are able to give a year-by-year estimate that will be meaningful if not totally reliable.

The chief factor affecting population projections is the fertility rate. Birth rates, by their very nature are highly volatile. It is usual therefore to consider future births under several headings.

1. Number of births on the assumption of nil migration after the starting date of projections:
      (a) births to women married only once
      (b) births to remarried women
      (c) illegitimate births
2. Effect of assumed net inward migration.

The expected female population of the country in each year up to the year ending the projection, must be stated, and their marital status, their age, and duration of marriage recorded. From these

---

[1] For full calculations and explanations see *Economic Trends*, May 1965.

statistics it is possible to make assumptions about the age of marriage, the likely duration of marriage, and the number of fertile years women will have. From these assumptions it is possible to calculate in turn the most important fact of all – the number of children likely to be born to these women. Again reference must be made to recent past experience.

Consideration is then taken of a number of background factors which will influence the fashion for family size. These include:

1. continuing rise of real income per head
2. improved standards in housing
3. fashion for larger families
4. falling age of puberty
5. possible effects of simpler contraceptive methods
6. possible effects of recent increases in immigration

Edwin Cannan: the theory of optimum population

Many theories of population have been advanced and it is worth looking at some of the most important.

Although Edwin Cannan's theory has been severely criticized since it was first put forward by Cannan in 1888 – and Cannan himself recognized certain inadequacies – it still forms the starting point for all economic analysis of the size of the population. The 'optimum population' is an equilibrium size towards which it would be beneficial for population of a given economy to grow and at which it should stabilize: to go further would lead to diminishing returns per head of population and a decline in the standard of living, elements which are involved in the concept of overpopulation. In strictly economic terms, optimum population is reached when the economy is producing at its most efficient, i.e. with maximum returns per head of population.

In broader terms it may be measured in terms of maximum economic welfare – which is much the same, but which has regard to questions of income distribution, as well as just the crude production of ever-increasing returns per head. Welfare may be taken as a measure of the ability of the economy to satisfy the needs of the population. When this concept is admitted it might be found that the optimum population may be smaller in an economy which is concerned with more equal distribution than in an economy primarily concerned with economic growth at all costs.

The concept of 'optimum population' makes use of an earlier theory – that of diminishing returns. Simply stated, this theory

7

relates increasing outputs to inputs, one of which is a fixed factor. As increasing inputs of a variable factor (say labour) are added to a fixed factor (say land) the output at first increases, but, after further additions of the variable factor, the returns per head of the variable factor tend to diminish and continue to diminish until the fixed factor can be increased. The classical economists used the concept of

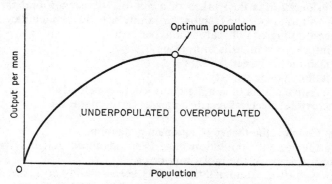

Fig. 1. *Returns to Population – concept of the optimum*

the law of diminishing returns to explain the progress of population growth relative to a position of optimum population. With optimum population conveniently measured in average returns per head of population, it is possible to see if average returns per head of population (the variable factor) are increasing or diminishing relative to the fixed factor (land and resources) and thus to select the point of optimum population where returns per head are at maximum.

But the concept of diminishing returns is essentially a short term view, in which one factor is fixed. In practice longer periods are important, where all factors are variable. The law of diminishing returns is applicable here too in a sense, but it is called the law of variable proportions, where all factors are variable, but some are more variable than others. It is the relation of those factors that are relatively fixed to those factors that are more easily varied that is important in the long period.

In the long run, the law of variable proportions states that if all factors are not increased proportionately, the resulting increase in output will be less than proportional. There will still be diminishing returns to the factor that has increased, because it is combining with fewer units than before of the other factors. These factors are thus

8

looked upon as being fixed relative to the increase in the other factors.

These factors might best be looked upon as 'scarce' factors, the increase in which takes some considerable time, whilst the other factors can be increased more easily. These scarce factors can be considered fixed during the period of time between one addition and the next. And then, if they are not added to in the same proportion as the variable factors, diminishing returns will become apparent.

The long-run trends will depend on the quality of the scarce factors. It could be that whilst short-term returns increase, the long-term trend is diminishing returns per head. For instance, in the case of agriculture the best land may be used first. As more land is brought into cultivation returns increase, but because the land is of poorer quality, the long-term trend is for diminishing returns to set in. If the additions to the scarce factors are of equal quality or even improving quality – as technical knowledge increases – then it is possible to obtain increasing returns.

The major fault with this theory is that it is an attempt to give an absolute point of equilibrium where no absolute point is possible. However it must be viewed still as a basic theory of demography, for the concept can still be used in a less rigid way. It provides a necessary tool of analysis when discussing problems of overpopulation and underpopulation, whose nature depends on the relationship between the size of the population and the resources available to sustain it.

Malthus and the theory of overpopulation

The theory of overpopulation is directly related to law of diminishing returns and the law of variable proportions, and to the concept of optimum population. As shown in Fig 1, if the level of population is giving returns per head which are increasing, the country is said to be underpopulated; if the returns per head are declining, the country is said to be overpopulated.

The theory of overpopulation will be dealt with in greater detail in Chapter 2. At this point it is only necessary to give a brief historical introduction of the theory as first conceptualized by the Reverend T. R. Malthus in 1798.

The Economist of December 31, 1967 reviewing the reissue of Malthus' *First Essay on Population*, published in 1798, said 'The first issue of this book has some claim to be the most influential book, excepting Marx on Capital, to be written in the last two hundred years . . .'

Malthus can be regarded as the founder of British demography. Although not quite the first writer in the field, his various editions of the *Essay on Population* captured the attention of Britain when they were first published, and to some extent still hold the imagination of society to-day. Malthus has been proved wrong in many instances but, like Cannan's theory of optimum population, there is enough in his theory, particularly the qualified theory developed later, for it to be used as a general law of economics.

Malthus' main hypothesis was simply that man's ability to reproduce himself, what Malthus called 'the passion between the sexes which appears to exist in as much force as it did two thousand or four thousand years ago', is greater than his ability to produce the means of subsistence.

This 'passion between the sexes' means that man's population would increase at a geometric progression every twenty-five years and the food supply would increase only at an arithmetic progression, thus leaving a demand and supply gap, which would, if not corrected, produce widespread famine, misery, illness and poverty. These misfortunes may bring the population back into some kind of equilibrium, but then the cycle would start again.

Malthus puts his case simply, but with impassioned vigour, typical of the nineteenth century clergyman he was:

> The necessary effects of these two different rates of increase, when brought together, will be very striking. Let us call the population of this island 11 millions; suppose that the present produce equal to the easy support of such a number. In the first twenty-five years the population would be 22 millions, and the food being also doubled, the means of subsistence would be equal to the increase. In the next twenty years the population would be 44 millions and the means of subsistence only equal to 33 millions. In the next period the population would be 88 millions, and the means of subsistence just equal to the support of half that number. And, at the conclusion of the first century, the population would be 176 millions, and the means of subsistence only equal to the support of 55 millions, leaving a population of 126 millions totally unprovided for.
>
> Taking the whole earth, instead of this island, emigration would of course be excluded; and, supposing the present population equal to a thousand millions, the human species would increase as numbers 1, 2, 4, 8, 16, 32, 64, 128, 256, and the subsistence as 1,

2, 3, 4, 5, 6, 7, 8, 9. In two centuries the population would be to the means of subsistence as 256 to 9; in three centuries as 4096 to 13 and in two thousand years the difference would be incalculable.

Malthus foresaw a very dismal end to this progression:

The ultimate check to population appears then to be a want of food, arising necessarily from the different ratios according to which the population and food increase. But this ultimate check is never the immediate check, except in cases of actual famine. Before this ultimate stage is reached disease will strike at mankind, causing death and great misery. Perhaps before this, man as a civilized being will have taken stock of his surroundings and taken action on his own.

The end being so dismal, Malthus predicted that a variety of preventive and positive checks would operate before the ultimate disaster overcame mankind. Man being a rational being would be able to look about him and see the dangers to his economic welfare occasioned by producing more children. He would make decisions and take action to avert the possible disasters. Malthus' proposals for preventing the too rapid growth of population may sound strange to our twentieth-century ears, for to some large extent his words have been misrepresented by disciples of population control. Nevertheless he still has something to say which is relevant.

Malthus' most important check was later marriage, or to use his own words, 'To prevent a great number of persons in all civilized nations from pursuing the dictate of nature in an early attachment to one woman'. He brushed aside the notion that such a control of man's natural urges would cause unhappiness and frustration by pointing out that it was the lesser of two evils. Malthus' other proposal was severe moral restraint. Not for him the control of birth by the use of contraceptives; such he abhored as being immoral.

Of positive restraints the restraint from marriage which is not followed by irregular gratifications may properly be called moral restraint. Promiscuous intercourse, with unnatural passions, violations of the marriage bed, and improper arts to conceal the consequences of irregular connexions, are preventive checks that clearly come under the head of vice.

In addition to the positive checks which man might use himself by conscious decision-making, Malthus foresaw a large variety of

11

'unwholesome occupations, severe labour and exposure to the seasons, extreme poverty, bad nursing of children, great towns, excesses of all kinds, the whole train of common diseases, and epidemics, wars, plague and famine' which would to some extent keep population growth in check.

Little wonder that he gained for economics the nickname of 'the dismal science'. Yet his writings are all too relevant in the present day. There cannot be much light in the life of two-thirds of the world's present population of 3,000 million who are suffering from malnutrition and endemic disease.

Marx and population

Marx, although writing close to the time of Malthus, took almost the opposite view of the problem of population. Whereas Malthus overemphasized the problem of overpopulation Marx declined to see it at all. Marx believed that if there was such a condition as overpopulation it was caused entirely by a fault of a capitalist society: that of maldistribution of resources. The problem could be solved easily enough by the reorganization of the social and economic structure and perhaps, if the country was territorially small, by expansion of land area. To Marx the wealth of society was the product of its labour. Therefore the greater supply of labour, the greater the wealth.

Written like this the Marxist theory of population may look absurd. But Marx's writings were truly revolutionary. Under a socialist system, he argued, with socialist planning and management, full use would be made of the resources of production, in particular the labour factor. In this way maximum returns per head would be achieved and population would be stabilized at the optimum. In this sense, and in this sense only, Marx declined to view overpopulation as a problem. Indeed countries such as China and the USSR, which have tried Marxist policies in practice, have demonstrated that the Marxist concept of increasing labour supply has been consistent with increasing returns to a great extent.

Neo-Malthusian theories

There are many theories which are described as Malthusian which would not be admitted as such by Malthus himself, were he alive to pass judgement. In particular, groups who advocate contraception as a positive check to population growth are not Malthusians in the

12

true sense of the word, because at no time did Malthus ever advocate or condone artificial birth-control.

Nevertheless groups have come into being advocating this policy and claiming to be Malthus' successors. The Malthusian League, founded late in the nineteenth century, opened its first birth control clinic in Walworth, in South London, in 1921 only a few months after the pioneering Marie Stopes Centre for Mothers.

More recently Malthusian principles have been applied to countries in Asia and Africa, where problems of overpopulation are most pressing. In 1961 Professor Richard Titmuss of the London School of Economics analyzed the problem of population in Mauritius with conclusions strongly reminiscent of the Malthusian interpretation. For instance

in the 30 year period ending in 1952 the population increased by 125,000 or 33 per cent . . . the birth rate is now over 25 per cent higher than it was in the 1930s . . . the rapid decline in mortality has contributed substantially to the growth of population . . . this means an addition to the population in fifteen years much larger than that actually experienced in Mauritius over the past 100 years . . . frankly, they amount to economic, social and political disaster. We would be failing in our duty if we used any other word. Already the national income of Mauritius is declining. What will the standard of living be like if the population more than doubles in the next twenty-five years?[1]

The problem was a microcosm of the Malthusian hypothesis and the language of the report is couched in suitably Malthusian tones. Only the remedies are not Malthusian for Professor Titmuss and his team recommended massive social welfare help and a comprehensive birth-control programme, along with other suggestions towards the improvement of agriculture and industry on the island.

Another group of neo-Malthusians of a more orthodox kind decry foreign aid to developing countries troubled with population problems. They argue that increasing aid, far from helping such countries, only serves to increase the problem by encouraging more births and reducing child mortality. The consequent population explosion may lead to aggressive nationalism and efforts at territorial expansion.

All modern forms of the Malthusian analysis argue that man has

---

[1] R. Titmuss, *Social Policies and Population Growth in Mauritius*, Cass, 1967.

it in his power to use the most positive check within the animal kingdom – that of contraception and careful family planning. This policy is difficult to put into practice in some states because of the political and religious difficulties involved. Even in Britain proposals for comprehensive contraceptive advice to be given free of charge on the National Health Service would face strong moral objections from many sections of the population.

Glossary of demographic terms

Total Population: the *de facto* population, plus H.M. forces serving overseas, minus the overseas forces resident in the United Kingdom.

Home, or Census, Population: the total number of persons actually living in the United Kingdom.

Natural Increase: the excess of births over deaths.

Birth Rate (Crude:) the number of live births in a given place over a given period, expressed as an average ratio per thousand of population. Birth Rate is calculated as:

$$\frac{\text{Total Births}}{\text{Total Population}} \times 1000$$

Age Specific Birth Rate: the number of births per thousand population at each age level. This is a much more useful figure than the crude birth rate because it indicates changes in population patterns.

Fertility Rate: the total of births per 1000 females in the fertility age-group, assumed to be 15–45 years.

Reproductive Rate: the extent to which females in the fertility age-ranges are replaced by the next generation.

Infant Mortality: the number of deaths of infants under the age of one year, expressed as a ratio of 1000 live births.

Death Rate (Crude): the number of deaths in a given place over a given period, expressed as an average ratio per thousand of population. Death Rate is calculated as:

$$\frac{\text{Total Deaths}}{\text{Total Population}} \times 1000$$

Age Specific Death Rate: the number of deaths per thousand population at each age level. Again this figure is more precise than the crude average.

Women at Risk: the number of women who are married and thus more open to risk of pregnancy. Care must be taken over this figure since women who are not married and who are within the age fertility range are also open to the risk of pregnancy. It is assumed, however, that married women are more likely to become pregnant. The child bearing age groups are taken to be 15–45 years.

Migration: a particular aspect of population study, involving movements of people from one place to another. If the movement takes place within a country, we talk of internal migration; if the movement is from one country to another, we talk of external migration.

Immigration: people coming to settle in a state from abroad.

Emigration: people leaving a state to settle in another country.

Age Distribution: the number of people in particular age groups throughout the population.

Sex Distribution: the number of people of each sex in particular age levels throughout the population.

Occupational Distribution: the number of persons occupied in particular trades, industries and professions within the economy.

Structure of Population: analysis of a population in terms of age distribution, sex distribution, occupational distribution.

Dependent Population: the number of persons not contained within the working population who are dependent on the production of others for their income.

Working Population: 'those gainfully employed of all ages and occupations including persons working on their own account as well as employees'. In fact this official definition is perhaps too narrow. The working population, includes all persons who are insured and registered for work. Thus students over the age of fifteen are not included in the working population, nor are men

15

and women retiring before the age of sixty-five, but men and women working beyond retiring age are, as are the members of the armed forces and those who are registered as unemployed.

Dependency Ratio: the ratio of working to non-working, or dependent, population.

CHAPTER 2
THE PRESSURE OF POPULATION

The pressure of population
Population pressure is a term which, taken by itself, is meaningless. To be useful, we must know what kind of pressure is being exerted, on what the pressure is being exerted, from which direction the pressure is coming, and what the likely effects of this pressure are, for both the economy and society.

The short answer is that population exerts pressure on the resources (the factors of production: land and labour, capital and entrepreneurship) of the economy. Pressure can be applied from two directions:

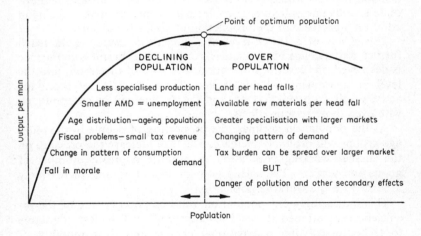

Fig. 2. *Effects of Overpopulation/Declining Population*

by increasing population or by decreasing population. If the population is increasing beyond the optimum point, the country is becoming overpopulated: if the population is falling from the optimum point, the country is experiencing a declining population, with all its

17

attendant consequences. Fig 2 sets out the likely economic effects of the different pressures of population.

Effects of a declining population

A population that is declining from the optimum will have a larger amount of land and resources, including capital equipment per head. The effect will be that production levels will decline – a function of there not being sufficient units of labour to benefit from full specialization or division of labour. This will mean that inefficiency will creep into industrial processes: the standards and levels of production will decrease as a result. The output per.head will fall; the real standard of living will fall and further secondary consequences will follow.

The reduced population will have a lower demand for all units of production, including food and building. One beneficial offshoot of this would be a reduction in the level of imports, but the net effect would not be good, in that the effect of a lower aggregate money demand (AMD) would be lower levels of employment and perhaps quite serious unemployment problems in particular areas, causing in addition a decrease in the production of goods for export.

The effects of a lower level of aggregate demand would reach further, and damage businessmens' confidence. If business confidence is destroyed, the level of innovation, the level of invention, and the level of investment will all decline. Thus, the level of economic activity will drop still further, and the decline will be compounded with even more serious effects.

As the population declines, the proportion of people in the older age groups will probably increase. This will increase the pressure on the smaller working population to produce a greater number of goods and services. The ageing population will become increasingly a burden on the working population.

This increasingly old population will compound some of the inefficiencies mentioned above. The older people will be less adaptable to technological and occupational change and their mobility of labour, geographical, industrial and occupational, will all be lower than a younger population.

Because older people form a larger proportion of the total population, they will fill a larger number of senior posts. The competition for promotion will therefore be much keener, but the degree of frustration will increase, making for a lower level of working morale and might contribute to an increasing rate of migration, as young people see job opportunities decreasing. Once again the effects are compounded.

The effects on macro-economic management are very serious: the larger number of dependants will increase the burden on public utilities, national debt, and social services. The increased burden on public utilities will spring from the large scale economies that the utilities – coal, rail, gas, electricity – gain from producing for a large population. Any serious decrease in this total would necessarily increase drastically the burden of their overheads. The proportion of fixed costs per unit would increase, helping to force up prices. The National Debt effect would be the same, for the burden of the Debt will be shared by a smaller number of people.

The most serious burden will come in the field of fiscal policy, where demand for more public social services will increase, whilst the community's ability to increase taxation to pay for this demand will be seriously impaired. As the population grows older, the number of pensions paid by the State will increase, the number of medical treatments will increase, all at the time when the money supplied by Social Security contributions will be smaller. Most important, the ability of the state to produce revenue in the form of taxation will be diminished.

So, with a declining population, there would be a widening budgetary gap which would have serious inflationary tendencies. A smaller working population would have to support a larger non-working population, and if it could not, either the standard of living under the Welfare State would have to be reduced or the Government would have to fill the gap either by taking more in taxation and social security contributions – which would increase the disincentive for people to produce and invest more – or by a budget deficit, which over a period of time would have serious inflationary effects.

These are the primary effects of a declining population. However, there are always secondary effects, which though relatively minor in their own right are often more persistent and in their aggregate effect are very damaging.

The secondary effects of a declining population centre around the morale of a population living in a society which does not have enough faith even to reproduce itself. In all parts of life, the standards and quality of that society's culture could diminish. As the population continued to decline, those who had faith in the future and in their abilities, and those who have inventions to offer, would leave and seek other locations, where their abilities would be better rewarded. The effect of the young, the virile, and the inventive leaving will be to leave the home economy in an even worse state than before, and will once again compound the effect of a declining population.[1]

Effects of overpopulation

The primary effects of overpopulation are the ones outlined originally in the Malthusian *Essay on Population*. They begin with the classic economic test of lower output per head, and go on to include malnutrition, poverty, disease, chronic and persistent unemployment, overcrowding and a breakdown of economic services.

The secondary effects are more concerned with the quality of life rather than the quantity. They include pollution; the psychological dangers brought about by high-rise living and urban overcrowding; a decline in educational and social services; the problems of environment, when rural amenities come into direct conflict with the need for increasing industrialization; the problems of urban environment, when the demands of traffic and problems make ordinary citizens less than important and sweep important amenities out of the way in the name of progress; the enormous fiscal problem grappled with by local and central government in their effort to meet demands raised in the name of progress; and finally the quality of life in terms of stability of relationships and individual privacy.

Lower output per head is a simple yardstick in theory but is very difficult to use in practice because of the large number of qualifications that have to be made concerning supply of resources, level of technological achievement, and the quality of labour force. However, it is still possible to make meaningful comparisons based on this concept by looking at output figures per head for, say, India, Mauritius and the United Kingdom over the last years. India and Mauritius are classic cases of overpopulation, whilst relatively speaking, Britain is a highly developed industrial economy with a balanced population.

---

[1] Readers are encouraged to refer to books explaining the fears of a declining population expressed during the inter-war period in Great Britain: *The Struggle for Population*, D. V. Glass; 'The Future Population of Britain', G. C. Leybourne, *Sociological Review*, April 1934; *The Population of Britain*, Eva M. Hubback, 1947.

Consider also the case of France between the Wars and Ireland in the second half of the nineteenth century.

G.N.P.	1958	1967	G.N.P. per head	1958	1967
India	$26,459m	$37,229m	India	$64	$73
Mauritius	$122m	$163m	Mauritius	$200	$211
U.K.	$52,331m	$87,310m	U.K.	$1,013	$1,586

The figures are even more startling when you compare distribution of income which is more uneven in India than Britain. This means of course that the poor in India are even poorer than the figures above imply. However, such comparisons give no absolute standard.[1] Judged by other standards, such as those involved in the secondary effects of overpopulation, it might be demonstrated that Britain itself is overpopulated.

Malnutrition and hunger

The Third World Food Survey concluded its report that 'as a very conservative estimate, some 20 per cent of the people in developing countries are undernourished and 60 per cent are malnourished.'[2] In other words, since well over half the world's population live in these areas, between 300 and 500 million people are not getting enough to eat.

The following table, based on information from eighty countries, compares the average calorie supply in different regions of the world with corresponding requirements. From the table the gap between demand and supply can be seen.

Area	Populations (1969) millions	Calorie supply per head	Calorie requirements per head
Europe	665	3,040	2,590
North America	211	3,110	2,590
Oceania	17	3,250	2,610
Far East	1,678	2,069	2,300
Near East	145	2,470	2,400
Africa	272	2,360	2,340
Latin America	237	2,510	2,410

[1] *U.N. Statistical Yearbook*, 1969.

[2] Oxfam, May 1967.

If calorific value does not mean much to the layman, he can gain a better understanding about what malnutrition means by studying comparative diets of children in different parts of the world.

Typical Diets of Children
Typical diets of 5-year-old British child

Breakfast	Dinner	Tea
½ oz. Cornflakes	2 oz. Stewed Steak	2 oz. Scrambled egg
5 oz. Milk	2 oz. Carrots	2 oz. Bread
1 oz. Bread	2 oz. Potatoes	4 oz. Apple
½ oz. Butter	5 oz. Milk ⎱ Milk Pudding	¾ oz. Butter
1 oz. Bacon	½ oz. Rice ⎰	½ oz. Jam
2 oz. Tomato		5 oz. Milk

Midmorning	Bedtime
5 oz. Orange Juice	5 oz. Milk

Child's diet (aged 2–5 years) in S. E. Asia

Breakfast	Lunch
1 bowl of parched or puffed rice	1 bowl of cold rice cooked previous
Brown sugar	night with mango pickle
Water	Cholli (green vegetables)
	½ oz. dried fish (2 or 3 times a week)

or
Piece of rice cake – plain or with brown sugar

Supper
1 bowl hot rice, vegetables (red pumpkin, eggplant)

Diet for children aged 2–5 in Africa

Plantain (similar to banana)	3oz.
Coco Yam (edible tubers)	10oz.
Cassava (tuber made into flour)	2oz.
Coco yam leaf	½oz.
Onions	¼oz.
Lean meat (beef, mutton, antelope)	¼oz.

Lima beans, Peanuts, Garden eggs, Peppers (red and green), Smoked Fish, Red Palm Oil in small quantities.
(Oxfam, November, 1969.)

The labour effect of overpopulation
The classic labour effect of overpopulation enumerated in the pages of elementary economic textbooks is unemployment. But the truth

drawn from the bitter experience of a modern community has more impact than the dry pages of a textbook. For this experience we turn again to India.

Today, India is judged a classic case of overpopulation. Yet, in 1946 at the time of Indian independence, conditions were relatively favourable for economic expansion compared with the other developing countries. A stable government, with a well-trained administration and a well-formed local government structure, officiated over an economy with all the basic essentials of a transport system, an educational system and some primary industries, that were well enough developed to be described as traditional. True, the Indian economy was basically agricultural, and low productivity agriculture at that, but there were supplies of coal, iron ore, and bauxite. This was more than other developing countries possessed. Why therefore has it become a classic case of underdevelopment and overpopulation?

Since independence India has been developing fast through a series of Five Year Plans. Between 1956-60, according to official estimates, the national income rose by 20 per cent. But the significant rise in national output has been largely neutralized by a demographic pressure, which even India's planners had not anticipated.

The population of India has been rising at an annual rate of more than 2 per cent. This very fast rate of increase, quite apart from cancelling out any real improvement in output, has created a problem of chronic unemployment. Neither of the first two economic plans managed to attain their targets with regard to employment, and in 1961 the number unemployed in India had risen to nine millions, whilst the number under-employed was estimated at between 15–18 millions. As an economist has commented recently 'The removal of unemployment thus remains "India's problem of problems".'[1]

This labour effect is further intensified when one considers the type of unemployment and the quality of the labour force involved. India is suffering from a shortage of jobs. The jobs that are being created by the developing economy are mainly in the developing industries, the investment industries and new manufacturing industries. Yet 70 per cent of India's population is illiterate, and is thus unable to participate in or contribute to these developing industries effectively.

Great though the efforts are to quicken the rate of educational

---

[1] M. Wegber, 'India', *Econ. Bulletin*, III, No. 2.

improvement, the chances of absorbing a low quality labour force into an economy which is trying to become increasingly specialized and scientific are low. The solution can only be over a long term; there are no short cuts.

Economic historians of the Industrial Revolution in the United Kingdom have asserted that the influence of a growing population on economic growth was beneficial and precipitated the upturn in all the industrial indices, which characterized that stage of British development. The pressure of population was sufficiently great to provide a stimulant, but not so great as to swamp progress. But in a country suffering from overpopulation, as India is. the pressure is so great that it may choke attempts to increase national output and economic growth.

As the increasing mass of the population feels that its governments are floundering under the constantly increasing pressure, economic instability may be translated into political instability, and the social fabric of the state may break into ever more self-centred interest groups, intent on their own solution to their own problem. In these circumstances the Malthusian predictions may come true.

The primary effects of overpopulation prophesied by Malthus a century and a half ago do not seem applicable to Britain today. But increasingly they are apparent on a world scale. The 1969 Reith Lectures were devoted to this theme of world population growth and its effects on man's environment; and Lord Ritchie Calder speaking in 1968 described the main problem facing the world as 'the problem of the world's ever-increasing population. A hair-raising forecast has been made, that within the lifetime of a child born today 15,000 million people would have to be fed and housed – nearly five times as many as now.'

Secondary effects of overpopulation

Yet the problem of overpopulation is increasingly relevant to Britain and other industrialised states. But it is not in primary terms that the effects are being analysed. The focus of the concern is the secondary effects of overpopulation, which lead to a deterioration of man's environment and the quality of his life.

The secondary effects of overpopulation are concerned with land use, the effect of different densities of population and the demands population places on the resources of the area. Man seeks to increase production from areas of agricultural land. In his search for greater

production pesticides, insecticides and fertilizers have been used –
this is one of the prime reasons why Malthus' original predictions
have not been realized – but in time these methods have produced
side effects which are very much less than beneficial. At Lake Clear,
California *all* wildlife around the lake died after being sprayed with
DDT. At Storm Lake, Iowa, a blue-green algae created by insecticides
killed 8,000 wild birds and animals.

Pollution is a single word that covers a great number of conditions.
When population densities are high the volume of effluence and
human waste to be disposed of is immense. If this sewerage is not
treated, rivers, seas, beaches and countryside become polluted, the
quality of the environment declines and natural life dies. The motor
car appears to have become the symbol of a consumer society; the
motor car satisfies many more consumer needs than the simple fact
of transportation. With this satisfaction comes pollution of the air
and the environment, which in some areas reaches such heights that
there is a danger to health. Pollution of the atmosphere, produced by
jet aircraft also gives cause for concern, as jet aircraft pump millions
of tons of poisonous carbon dioxide into the air every year. The
Rhine carries 12,000 tons of oil waste per day. Lake Erie has accumu-
lated sediment 30″ – 125″ thick over an area of 10,000 sq. miles.
Flights of jet aircraft over New York emit thirty-six million tons of
carbon dioxide annually. 12,000 tons of waste are pumped into Los
Angeles air each day from car exhausts. New York produces seven
million tons of human waste per year: 1,000 tons per hour.

Lastly, there is the growing problem of urban growth. This is
much greater than a direct conflict between land for urban sprawl,
industrial use, agricultural use and leisure use; the relevance of urban
growth to population growth goes much deeper. The relevance has
been stated so far in terms of physical outputs which are not beneficial to the environment. In addition, scientists are becoming increasingly aware that the nature of life in urban communities or, 'close
living' as it is called, may cause stress, cardiac arrest, and depressive
illnesses all of which may lead to premature death, or to anti-social
behaviour, which in turn sets up community conflicts. Much research
has been done on overcrowding in the animal world by American
scientists.[1] Their findings have sufficient parallel with human experience to act as a warning.

It would be incorrect to ascribe all the effects described above to

---

[1] See Gordon Rattray Taylor, *The Doomsday Book*.

population growth alone. Economic growth and the increasing demand from societies for higher standards of living are as much to blame as population growth. But the two travel hand in hand. More people require more goods, and rich people require and demand even more goods than poor people. So the pressure of population is compounded by the pressure from an affluent society.

Since the beginning of the Industrial Revolution, Britain's economy and those of the other developed countries of the world, have become used to working for industrial, economic and commercial expansion. In certain periods of history growth was pursued 'at all costs'. In the peak years of Victorian expansion little thought was given to the environment or the people in it, and no thought at all was given to the future population or their environment. It was assumed that if the businessmen could produce the increasing volume of goods and services needed by the economy, that was sufficient justification. It is only recently that the economic notion of social cost has entered into calculations. During the 1930s Professor Pigou drew attention to the indirect costs to society resulting from business decisions. It has taken a generation for this concept to be quantified but during the 1960s a system of cost-benefit analysis emerged whereby the full cost of business decisions could be accounted, based on the cost to society of the side effects of business decisions. A monetary value was established, consistent with the value that the economy would place on the bi-products. As a result, it is now possible to have a much more definite idea of the opportunity cost – expressed in the secondary effects of population growth – involved in population and economic growth.[1]

---

[1] For further reading, students are recommended to read, E. J. Mishan, *The Costs of Economic Growth.*

CHAPTER 3
THE BRITISH POPULATION

The growth of British population is best examined in five separate periods. Population trends and the major causes of growth can then be isolated, and high-lighted.

From the Domesday Book to 1700

Domesday Book (1086) was not in itself a population study. It was a national income study undertaken by William the Conqueror to estimate the wealth of his new kingdom. But because this involved counting households and their belongings, it can be taken to be the first census ever conducted in this country. That is not to say that it was in every way accurate, for there were many omissions, and the final report was guilty of inaccuracies and double-counting, but allowing for these, the population of England was between $1\frac{1}{2}$ and $1\frac{3}{4}$ millions at this time, largely living south of a line joining the Wash with the Bristol Channel, the north being, to quote Daniel Defoe at a much later date, 'the wildest part of the country'.

Throughout the whole period, both birth and death rates were very high – it is estimated that birth rates were in the region of 32–45 per thousand, and death rates around 30–40 per thousand, but the rate of growth of population, being fairly typical of early agricultural economies, was low, around 0·5 per cent to 1·0 per cent per annum. There were of course wide annual divergences from these average figures, and at times, as during the Black Death, the death rate rose to as much as 300 per thousand.

Infant mortality was high throughout, which meant that the pressure on the family was to give birth to as many children as possible. With famine, epidemics and plague a constant hazard, the life expectancy in Britain was very low, equivalent to that of Borneo today – about twenty-eight years. With the death rate only slightly lower than the very high birth rate, population growth was slow. But it was steady, and by the middle of the fourteenth century had reached about three millions. The Black Death was the most dramatic single influence on population in this period. The years 1348–49 saw the total population cut by about a third, the gradual trend of the last 280 years stopped, and the level of population reversed almost to the 1086 position. The plague returned in severe epidemics on several occasions in the fourteenth and fifteenth centuries, but the old trend was re-established, and according to a survey conducted by Gregory King, the population of England and Wales reached between five and six millions by the end of the seventeenth century. Scotland was populated by a further one million people so that the total population of the United Kingdom at this time was near seven million.

The eighteenth century: 'sustained growth'

In English demographic history, the eighteenth century is often linked with the nineteenth century as a single period. This is a pity. The eighteenth century contains the major sources of population change, and the fact that in the third quarter of this century both

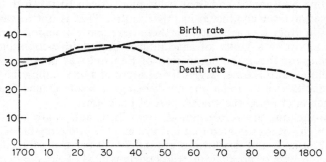

Fig. 3. *Average birth and death rate per 1,000 per decade*

the population and the economy achieved 'sustained growth' at around the same time is of sufficient significance to rate a more intensive study. Indeed, the eighteenth-century growth, for long considered easily explainable in demographic terms, is now the focus of academic controversy.[1] The causes of this demographic revolution are particularly important for the Industrial Revolution, with which it is intimately linked.

The total population of England and Wales expanded from about

---

[1] For a brief survey of controversy see: M. W. Flinn, *Origins of the Industrial Revolution*; M. W. Flinn, *British Population Growth – 1700– 1850*. Dr. Flinn gives a comprehensive bibliography of authors who are involved in the controversy.

5·8 millions in 1701 to 11·9 millions in 1801, the date of Britain's first official census, at a rate of 15 per cent per decade, which must be compared with a growth rate of 5 per cent per decade during the preceding century. Growth rates were not steady throughout, but fluctuated, reacting to the social and economic stimuli of the times. Growth rates during the early decades were similar to medieval rates, but those later in the century, after 1741, speeded up, and increased progressively through into the nineteenth century.

It is important to remember that the birth and death rate statistics of the eighteenth century are only estimates, Drawn as they are from parish registers, inevitably they include many errors. But they are the only statistics we have, and as such we must value them. Birth rates increased from 31·6 in 1701 to 36·9 in 1741 and thereafter increased more slowly to an estimated eighteenth century peak of 37·7 in 1781. The death rate began by rising from 28·6 to 33·0 in 1741, having reached a peak of 35·8 in 1731. Thereafter it declined to 26·9 in the last decade of the century.

The traditional explanation of population growth during this period is that natural increase occurred because of reductions in the death rate, this in itself the result of improvements in medical knowledge, sanitation and public health, reflected particularly in a rapid decrease in infant mortality.

The eighteenth century saw the building of major schemes such as Guy's Hospital and Dr Coram's Foundlings Hospital, both in London, and even in some of the larger provincial cities some development in hospital building was going on. Improvements were certainly achieved in sanitation and public building. Nobody who has studied the early development of our cities, particularly such Georgian centres as London, Bristol, Newcastle and Bath can fail to notice the vast improvements in architecture, usage of materials, public sanitation and public buildings throughout the whole of the century, although the major developments came towards the end, with the full flowering of the Regency period. This improvement in the general condition of living had effects on the standard of health enjoyed by the population as a whole, and there was some improvement in infant mortality rates, with consequent spin-off effects on birth and reproductive rates.

Recently, however, this simplified view of death rate fluctuations has been seriously criticized.

The major qualification that must be admitted to the traditional death-rate explanation is that, though there were improvements, the effects were only marginal in the eighteenth century, although later, they added to the general forces of population growth.

The most important medical improvements came during the nineteenth century, with the application of Jenner's vaccine for smallpox (1798), improvements by Pasteur and Morton on anaesthetics, and Lister's work on post-operative infections. There were few really important discoveries during the early eighteenth century, and even the hospitals, important though they were to be in the future, were as often as not, harbourers of germs and disease, as much as they were healers in these early days. Some medical historians even believe them to have increased the death rate rather than lowered it.

Although improvements in sanitation and public buildings in the town must have improved health, it should be noted that only 30 per cent of the population were urban dwellers. Again the really important improvements came later, in the nineteenth century.

There was a decline in infant mortality, but the effects were marginal in the extreme, and they remained so until well into the twentieth century. In 1900 the infant mortality rate was as high as 145 per thousand, but by 1950 it had fallen to 35 per thousand.

Fluctuations in death rate *can* be explained in economic terms. Habakkuk has stressed the importance of a fitter people than before, saying that 'a people who survived the repeated plagues of the seventeenth century could survive anything, and, extending the "survival of the fittest" theory, they would beget fitter and fitter children in the future.'[1] But why were they fitter if medical improvements had only a marginal effect?

Legislation passed in 1707 and 1709 enforced new standards of building. Wood gave way to stone and brick, and on the roof, slate replaced thatch. During the medieval period rats carried the plague from township to village causing severe fluctuations in population growth. Rats and other vermin, throve in wooden buildings and thatch roofs and they found the new stone and brick buildings not so well to their liking. A direct result was a reduction in the incidence of plague, which had already suffered a major 'clean-up' in the Great Fire of London in 1666, and other infectious diseases.

There was a marked increase in life expectancies of men and women during this period. Since this is a contributory factor in

---

[1] H. J. Habakkuk, 'English Population in 18th Century', *Econ. Hist. Review*, 1953.

increasing family size and birth rate, it is important. Life expectancies are a function of health and sanitation and in this period they do reflect better personal hygiene and diet. The decades of 1720–50 were times of good, plentiful harvests. The good harvests caused food prices to fall, giving increasingly beneficial diets for labourers and farmworkers – the majority groups in the population These better diets were further affected by the effects from the Agrarian Revolution, in which improvements in cattle breeding, sheep breeding, planting of new crops, such as the nutritious potato, and efforts in rural drainage and hedging increased production. All these led to improvements in diet and hence in the health of the population.

From 1760 onwards, geographical regions of the country were increasingly linked to form a national market. The rapid growth in canal building, starting with the Bridgwater Canal near Manchester in 1761 continued to the early years of the nineteenth century. Then a new fever – that of steam engines and railways – gripped the nation! Both these technological innovations speeded up communication and travel. A national transport system meant that food could be switched quickly about the country and this decreased the number of local famines. Ease of transport reduced costs which in turn contributed to the relative fall in basic food prices.

A national market also encouraged the growth of industry. Regions of the country found it profitable to specialize in certain types of production. From Yorkshire and Lancashire came cheaper wool and cotton garments, and from Staffordshire, Derbyshire and Nottinghamshire the goods of the hosiery trade. Cheaper clothes, and more easily washed garments, also improved general health. The newly established chemical industry produced better soaps, thus contributing to the improvements in personal cleanliness and the general level of health. Even small improvements in these areas of human life produced, in consequence, longer life-expectancies.

Death rates and birth rates are related parts of the same mechanism, both having influence on the other, and both reacting to the same economic stimuli. Improvements in health and increased life expectancies must have had effect on attitudes to life and to family size and thus on birth rates.

The most important fact explaining the high birth rate, which reached a peak in 1781, and which remained high throughout the century, is the decline in the age of marriage.

Changing economic factors made it possible for young men and women to marry earlier. Opportunities for employment, the decline in tied apprenticeships, the general rise in money wages, all meant that young people gained a measure of economic independence earlier in life and this enabled them to set up home earlier than they had been able to do before. The evidence of Dr Wrigley, in his extensive researches in the population statistics of the village of Colyton in Devon, produces these facts about changing marital ages:[1]

> From 1720 onwards the mean age of women at first marriage declined slowly but steadily until the end of the century it had passed from almost 30 to 26 . . . In the period 1647–1719 only 4 per cent of all brides marrying for the first time were in their teens; in the period 1825–37, 25 per cent of these brides were teenagers. In the former period 10 per cent of all brides were in their forties when they first married; in the latter only 2 per cent were.

The increased period of married life during which women were fertile produced immediate effects on the birth rate. The average number of children of a couple marrying in their early twenties may well have been twice as many as a couple marrying in their thirties and even greater than a couple marrying in their forties. With the increasing longevity of women, greater life expectancy generally, and better health throughout a longer life, the number of women 'at risk' in their fertile years increased quite markedly during this period.

The Agrarian changes which increased the general health of the population also increased the possibility of having larger families. Food was cheap. More money was left over from spending on basic necessities which allowed families to think in terms of having another child. As the Industrial Revolution gathered pace, the increase in opportunities for employment, in particular child employment, meant that children became to some extent income earners rather than a cost on the family, and this further encouraged the growth in family size. Royston Pike in *Human Documents of the Industrial Revolution* pays great attention to the development of child labour, and he cites cases of children working at the age of four and even

---

[1] E. A. Wrigley, 'Marriage and fertility in Pre-Industrial England', *The Listener*, February 10th, 1966. Dr. Wrigley asserts that these changes occurring in Colyton are typical of changes that were occurring throughout pre-industrial Europe.

three years of age. At the same time the Speenhamland system of poor relief gave some families a subsidy towards family upkeep.

Dr M. W. Flinn writes, 'It is difficult to explain a significant rise in the birth rate in a pre-contraceptive era in other than economic terms'. To a large extent this is true. But there is evidence that some form of family planning was being used in England at this time, even though it was of fairly elementary kind. So much is heard of birth control today that one is apt to think of it as purely a twentieth century phenomenon. This is far from true. Contraception is mentioned in the Kahun Papyrus of 1850 BC, in the Bible, in Herodotus and in the writings of Fallopius. It was well-known to the aristocrats of France and Italy and appliances are mentioned by Lord Rochester (1647–80) and were advertized for sale in London as early as 1776. Coitus interruptus was no doubt the most common method, but research in French and English parishes makes clear that there was also elementary knowledge of the menstrual cycle . . . 'already those baneful secrets unknown to all animals but man have penetrated into the country places; they cheat nature even in the villages."

So the eighteenth century saw the British population well on course for a population explosion that was to occur in the next century. Interest largely centres on the causes of this sustained growth. It is evident that only in the latter part of the century could the decline in death rate be responsible for population growth. Growth in the early decades was definitely accounted for by an appreciable increase in birth rate, and during the middle decades and thereafter, both forces were moving in the same direction to produce accelerating rates of increase.

The nineteenth century: 'population explosion'

This period of very rapid population growth is a good deal simpler to explain than that of the eighteenth century.

Birth rate continued to increase until about 1875, whereafter it fell. Death rate fell throughout, and at an increasing pace from the middle of the century.[1]

The increase in birth rate in the first 80 years of the century is explicable in terms of the causes which set the birth rate on its upward trend in the previous period. The same factors were present but now

---

[1] *Origins of the Industrial Revolution*, M. W. Flinn. R. M. Grant, 'Demographic Approach to Social and Economic History', *Economics*, Spring 1965.

their effect was more pronounced as a result of the increasing economic activity following the transport and power revolutions of the 1780s and the Railway Revolution of the 1840s.

With increasing opportunities for both adult and child employment, household income increased, and with this increase in the

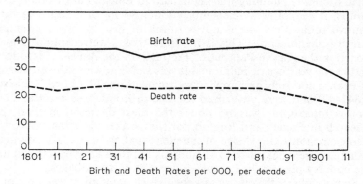

Fig. 4. *Population Explosion 1801–1913*
(The Registrar General)

general standard of living the age of marriage fell still further. 'In the early nineteenth century it [the age of marriage] fell still further, and much faster. By the 1820s and '30s it was only 23, so that in a period of 100 years the average age of women at first marriage fell by about seven years. This is an extraordinary transformation.'[1]

In addition to increases in the number of women at risk this further lowering of marital age had a marked effect on family size, and in the mid-decades of the Victorian period, the average number of children per family increased to between 5·5 and 6.

In this century the changes in death rate were much more influential than during the eighteenth century. Important improvements were made in medical knowledge, public health, and sanitation. The hypotheses which have been rejected as reasons for eighteenth century growth were now truly operative. A marked decline in infant mortality can be noted in the later decades, a result of improvements in clothing, food, housing, and medical knowledge. Cheap corn imports from America in the 1860s further increased the progress

---

[1] E. A. Wrigley.

34

made in improved diet by the agrarian and industrial innovations at home.

An interesting question is raised by the fairly sudden decline in the birth rate after 1870, when according to the theories so far put forward, with increasing standards of living, the birth rate should have continued at its high level of around thirty-five per thousand. The fact that by the turn of the century it had dropped to thirty is of some importance.

The standard answer to this question is that birth control became respectable and widely practised. Whilst there is some evidence of this, it is too simple an answer, and does not stand close examination. As we have seen from our studies of the eighteenth century, contraception is a means to an end, not an end in itself. It is the wishes of men that are important here.

There is some evidence that birth control was increasing. References to contraceptive appliances and techniques become more frequent at this time. James Mill refers to them in an article of 1818, and again in 1822; Francis Place recommends contraceptive techniques in his book *Illustrations and Proofs of the Principles of Population* and Richard Carlile in his pamphlet of 1825 *Every Woman's Book or What is Love* tries to persuade people to the process of family limitation. Birth control appliances were being used and were on sale quite early in the century, but it was not until the celebrated *Regina v. Bradlaugh – Besant* trial of 1876, in which a manual on birth control techniques was ruled obscene, that full publicity was focused on the subject. Even with this nation-wide publicity, birth control had very little effect on the immediate birth rate for it was practised largely by the middle and leisured classes who anyway had smaller families than the average.

Even among these groups it was certainly far from widespread (remember the almost adolescent excitement of the younger Forsytes in Galsworthy's *Forsyte Saga*, discussing their use of birth control – and that was in the 1920s). For the rest, family limitation relied on the old method of coitus interruptus – and that is by far the most accident prone method of contraception.

The reasons behind the movement towards smaller families must be explained by economic circumstances. With wage levels rising and the general level of the standard of living improving, legislation had been passed which made child employment illegal, and child education compulsory (several Factory Acts during the nineteenth century and the Education Act of 1870). Such legislation increased very considerably the cost of large families.

This has to be linked with the first symptoms of an affluent consumer society. Walk into any poster shop today and you will find displayed reproductions of early advertisements for tobacco, soap and other standard items of domestic expenditure. Examine the dates when the large London stores were founded – Harrods in 1849, Liberty's in 1875, William Whiteley, London's first custom built departmental store, in 1863, Selfridges in 1909, and of course those middle-class establishments – the Civil Service Stores and the Army and Navy Stores. These are signs of increased wealth and leisure, all alternatives which made people stop and weigh the economic consequences of having another child. Increasingly men and women chose the leisured alternative rather than give birth to another child which would add an increased burden of costs to the family.

Women began to agitate for emancipation which meant increasing pressure within the home for fewer children and more leisure for the woman of the household. The birth rate declined and continued to decline through the early years of the twentieth century to World War One, when there was a slight upward turn in the rate, only for it to return to its late nineteenth century trend as soon as the war was over.

1911–1939: declining population?
Years before the outbreak of the Second World War, concern with the British population and its future trends had been evident. At times during the 1930s there were fears that Britain was in the grips of an actual decline in population.

There was evidence to support this view. During the early twentieth century crude birth rate fell from 30 per thousand in 1901, to 24 in 1911 to 16 in 1931. Crude death rate continued to decline from 18 per thousand at the beginning of the century to 16 in the 1930s. This discernible slowing of the population growth assumed, to some people, alarming proportions. The then Chancellor of the Exchequer, Neville Chamberlain, said in the 1935 Budget Speech in which he introduced an increase in family allowances, 'I must say that I look upon the continued diminution of the birth rate in this country with considerable apprehension', and Professor A. M. Carr-Saunders, stated quite categorically in the introduction to his book, *The Struggle for Population*, 'The population of this country has now almost reached its peak; decline will shortly set in, and even if fertility remains at its present level, that decline will soon become rapid.'

The reasons for these developments have already been outlined for the previous period, but now they operated with increasing pressure.

The Royal Commission on Population set up in 1949 stated that the increased use of, improvements in, and availability of birth

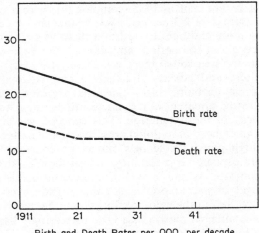

Birth and Death Rates per OOO, per decade

Fig. 5. *Period of Declining Population? 1913–39*
(The Registrar General)

control appliances was the most important single factor affecting limitation of family size in the period to the beginning of the Second World War.[1] That increased use of appliances, and social acceptance of deliberate methods of family limitation was important is not disputed, but it should be underlined again, that contraception is merely a means to an end, and the reasons behind the desire to use birth-control methods are more significant than the fact that birth control was used increasingly.

The forces which directly influenced families to limit the number of their children follow very much the pattern of the late Victorian period, but they were given greater effect by the social upheaval

[1] Royal Commission on British Population – Command 7695.

occasioned by the First World War, and by the Depression which followed.

We have already seen that families were beginning to think in terms of a smaller number of children from 1870 onwards, largely because children were now a cost on the family, rather than an income earner. The effect of the general depression, when wage levels dropped dramatically, and unemployment remained at an average level of 10 per cent of insured workers, and reached an all-time peak of 23 per cent in 1933 (compare this with a post Second World War average of 2·3 per cent) was to increase the cost-burden of producing more children. In addition there was a severe housing shortage throughout the period, and, though the beginnings of the Welfare State assisted some, there were many thousands who lived in abject misery and poverty. Further to emphasize the effect of economics on a declining birth rate, the aspiration to a higher standard of living, apparent in the nineteenth century, was now held by the majority of the population. This concept was given further force by the emergence of national press media and national advertising, which highlighted whole new ranges of consumer goods. In this social atmosphere large families, indeed families at all, became a social handicap, as the Royal Commission made plain: 'the discouragement of parenthood is not due to improved standards, but to the fact that, in the enjoyment of them, the parent, compared with the unencumbered person, has been increasingly handicapped.'

The First World War had two major effects on population trends. The most obvious effect was to kill 745,000 of the country's younger men, and to wound or mutilate 1·6 million more. These men amounted to about 9 per cent of the male population under the age of 45, and the slaughter produced a significant effect on the balance between the sexes, and on the size of the age groups who were concerned with marriage and child-bearing. This effect would be cumulative for there would be a greater number of women in the marriageable age groups without a man as the years went by, contributing further to an already declining reproductive rate.

The second effect, and the one that was already apparent, though less powerfully, before the war was the realization by women of their changing status and role in society. The Representation of the People Acts of 1918 and 1928, giving women the right to vote, and the emergence of 'The Flapper', are political and social manifestations of women's new role which included a right to be heard, both inside and outside the family unit. The importance of women's status inside the family unit is more important for our studies. It is fair to say that the feeling among women that they were much more than mere child bearers, received important support when they took up their place alongside men in the industrial structure, not merely as units of labour – as some women had always been from the birth of the Industrial Revolution onwards – but as responsible workers in jobs giving them economic and social status. It is not surprising therefore, that the formula of marriage changed somewhat, and women began asking for voluntary agreements within marriage on their role in the family and the consequent family size.

In this context the fashion for families is important. In all periods of history social example and imitation plays a major role, but it becomes increasingly important when mass media has developed to the point where opinions can be spread nationwide very quickly. The fashion for the more limited family must have been disseminated by the popular press, radio, public education, the cinema, advertising, and all the other forms of easier communication which brought into contact geographical and social groups to a greater extent than before.

After the Second World War: the population bulges

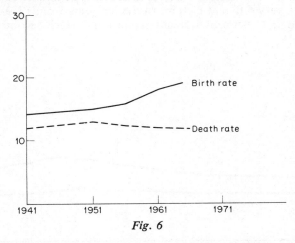

Fig. 6

The immediate post-war period saw a continuation of decline in the death rate, which began first in 1741, and two periods of increase in birth rate, the first between 1942 and 1947, the second during 1955–64.

39

The decline in population, threatened during the 1930s, did not occur. The death rate continued its steady decline, but in 1942 the first rise in the birth rate since 1880 occurred. This continued during the war years and into the immediate post-war period to 1947, by which time the rate had climbed to 20·7 per thousand. Thereafter, the rate declined again and it seemed that the pre-war trend was beginning to re-assert itself. Renewed fear of a declining population was reflected in the setting up of a Royal Commission on Population in 1949.

Between 1955 and 1964 the birth rate again began to climb, causing the second population bulge. Although the rate of population growth during this period – 0·45 per cent per annum – was slow compared with past experience, and compared with the world growth rate of 2 per cent per annum, it was still fast enough to cause concern amongst some economists and politicians that Britain might pass its optimum population level.

It is usual to dismiss the death rate as being less dramatic in effect within the British context, because of the relatively small decrease in recent years. Although the crude death rate has shown only small changes, a more detailed study of death rates in specific age groups, reveals a very different picture. In the ten years from 1950–60 there occurred an 11 per cent decrease in mortality, which becomes greater

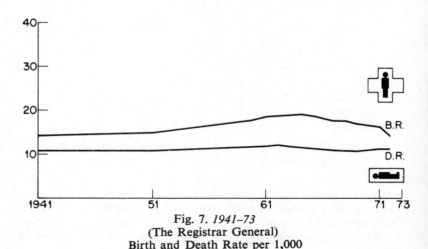

Fig. 7. *1941–73*
(The Registrar General)
Birth and Death Rate per 1,000

when age structure is taken into account. The really important change in mortality has been in the decrease in infant mortality and in the younger age ranges, which have cumulative effects on the rate of growth by increasing the chances of survival of those born. The number of deaths of children aged five or below has fallen from 205,000 in 1871, to 24,000 in 1951, to 18,000 in 1972. Even more striking has been the change in infant mortality, from a death rate of 145 per thousand in 1900 to 30 per thousand in 1951 and still further to 17 per thousand in 1972.

Yet this apart it is fluctuations in the birth rate which has attracted most attention, and it is these fluctuations which will be most important for future population growth.

The social background of the early post-war period was similar in outline to the pre-war period. Although there are important differences in levels of standards of living between the periods, there is a basic similarity in that the social objectives were the same, although in the post-war period, because of the emergence of a consumer society and the Welfare State, their achievement was a great deal easier. The continuing emancipation of women was another trend, re-establishing itself and developing further in the post-war period. In the search for higher social status and a higher material standard of living, the childless couple was obviously better placed than the couple with one, two or more children. This was true in the 1930s and it can be assumed that the social mores carried this concept through the war period, and into the 1940s. To a large extent this explains the decline in birth rate following the dramatic post-war bulge of 1946–48. With the economic atmosphere of the period being one of austerity, limitation of family size was an advantage in the social game of 'Keeping up with the Jones'. Declining birth rates during the later 1940s were therefore expected, and as the country's standard of living improved, it was anticipated that this trend would continue. This was the opinion of the Royal Commission of Population and other experts, including the Registrar General, who predicted a relatively slow growth of population growth in the last quarter of the twentieth century, leading to a population of sixty-three million by the year 2000.[1]

That this trend was changed by the increase in the birth rate in the mid 1950s was remarkable to the experts at the time, particularly when one considers the relatively small number of women in the

---

[1] Barbara Marlowe, *Charting the British Economy*, Longmans.

major fertility age groups, which was in turn a direct consequence of the lower birth rates of the 1930s. Changing economic conditions which influenced social attitudes and actions largely explain the change. The most important contrast between the economic situation of the 1950s and 1960s and that of the 1920s and 1930s, was the dramatic drop in the level of unemployment. If one takes the level of 'full employment' to be consistent with a 2 per cent unemployment rate, Britain enjoyed continuous full employment from the end of the war until the early 1970s. As can be seen from Fig. 7 this low figure compares with an average of 10 per cent for the corresponding period after World War One.

This, together with a general upward movement in wages and salaries, contributed towards a rapid increase in the general material standard of living, which, because of the growth of the system of progressive taxation and the development of the Welfare State encompassed many more millions of people than hitherto. For the vast majority the standard of living had never been higher, and Prime Minister Macmillan's 1959 pre-election slogan 'You've never had it so good' was not far from the truth.

The Welfare State had an important influence on the fashion for family size. The direct costs of child bearing to the individual family

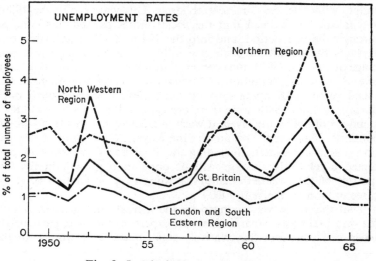

Fig. 8. *Level of Employment 1950–65*

have decreased from £15 (and this for doctor's fees alone) in 1930 when a working man's wage was 30s per week to almost nil. Increased maternity grants for all mothers and family allowances for the second, third and fourth children, in addition to free hospital and medical treatment and free education, have made the burden of a family much less than heretofore. This has cut into the advantage held by the childless couples during the previous period, and has done much to change the answer to the question 'Shall we have a (another) child?' from 'no' to 'yes'. Very often it is not a choice between leisure and a family: many modern affluent families can afford both; although there will always be an opportunity cost.

These changes in economic stimuli have contributed towards changes in social fashion, which has in turn produced changes in the fashion for family size from 2·0 to 2·5 children per family. Good employment opportunities, high levels of earnings and good possibilities that this trend would continue, have all meant a lowering of the age of marriage, and a rise in the number of marriages. These facts have resulted in a longer fertility period, and the possibility of greater number of pregnancies. This effect has been the more dramatic because of the greater independence and higher earnings of men *and* women in their late teens and early twenties. The age of marriage has been lowered ever further than it might have been, had only the adult population benefited from this changed economic atmosphere. In 1935 only 10 per cent of men and women marrying were under twenty; in 1965 the figure was 33 per cent; and this proportion is likely to increase during the next decade.

These changes, combined with a marked decline in the age of puberty, have resulted in a lowering of the age for child bearing, which is evidenced by statistics provided by the National Council for the Unmarried Mother – in 1960 the number of girls having babies below the age of fifteen was 588, and in 1966 it was 970. With men and women marrying earlier it is likely that completed family size will be bigger than if couples married in their late twenties and thirties.

No mention has yet been made of birth control and its increasing use during a period of sexual permissiveness and questioning of established moral codes. The availability of chemical and mechanical methods of contraception has increased vastly in recent years. The discovery of 'the pill' and the intra-uterine device has widened the use of contraception as socially acceptable behaviour to many thousands of people who previously reacted against use of the sheath or cap. Altogether some 284,000 people attended Family Planning Association clinics in Britain in 1961. The table reproduced on page 101 charts the increasing acceptance of family planning.

There are two ways of looking at this changing social behaviour and its effects on population growth. The first is that increased use of contraceptives has decreased the potential speed of population growth, for without them but with the increased standard of living enjoyed by all the population, increases in birth rate would have been even greater.

The second way of looking at the increased use of birth control methods is that without them the population may have returned to the pre-World War Two level for small families because the social pressures towards enjoying greater material benefits would have still benefited the childless couples more than those with children. With contraceptives and proper family planning, couples are able now to so plan their families that the birth of another child is already accounted for by increased family income, and families can be increased at times when the birth of a child is an asset to the family – in terms of enjoyment and satisfaction – and is in no sense a liability. In more cases the new born child can be planned and wanted and is not just an unfortunate mistake.

In this respect one more social factor of great importance must be mentioned. That is the increasing proportion of young women who marry early and who intend to continue working, until the birth of their first child – itself postponed by the use of effective family planning – and to resume their chosen careers at some later stage. In this, the whole conception of marriage has changed from a mere child bearing institution to one of setting up a joint home for satisfactory cohabitation without necessarily increasing the family size.

In all these trends, we see that the continued growth of natural increase has been a reaction against the small families of the 1930s, but in no sense a tendency to revert to the large families of Victorian times.

Natural increase accounted for the growth of British population in this post war period to a large extent, but it has been helped by a changing pattern in the migration. Throughout the twenties and thirties the United Kingdom was, on balance, a net emigrant population. This had also been the case during the nineteenth century as young men set forth to find their fortune in an expanding Empire, but in the 1950s the situation changed. With the development of a predominantly independent Commonwealth, the United Kingdom attracted immigrants from all parts of the Commonwealth, particularly from the Asian countries, Africa and the West Indies. Until 1962 there was no form of immigration control and increasing numbers of immigrants, both white and coloured, came to Britain to make it their home. A peak was reached in 1961 when the net immigration was 160,000 but since the passing of the Commonwealth Immigrants Act of 1962, this number has steadily fallen, until in 1966, Britain became a net emigrant country again. She has remained so ever since with a net outflow varying from 95,000 in 1966 to 39,000 in 1972. Nevertheless, considerable numbers of immigrants have moved into Britain – approximately one million between 1954 and 1963 – and the effect of this factor, while increasing the population in the short term may also have considerable importance for population developments and policy in the longer term.

From 1964 towards zero population growth

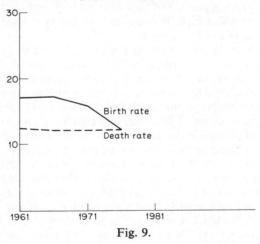

Fig. 9.

Changes in population over a period of time are caused by a combination of changes in death rate, birth rate, and the level of migration into and out of a country. Death rate maintained its known, and expected trend during the period, being almost stable from 12·5 in 1964 to 12·0 in 1976; the migration figures returned, in 1962, to a net outflow and continued thus; the most significant change – and in some respects the least expected by some observers – was the drop

45

in birth rate from 18·4 in 1964 to 11·9 in 1976, a fall which, in 1976, produced zero population growth in the United Kingdom for the first time in modern times.

The change to zero population growth, after half a generation of increasing population was as dramatic as it was unexpected. Making the assumption that population growth would decline once the effects of the world war had subsided, and having been proved wrong in this assumption by the baby boom of the 1955–64 period, it was thought not unlikely that the population would continue to increase to the end of the century. Indeed, in the first edition of this book, official 1971 estimates of population size through to the year 2001 suggested an upper figure of 73 million and a lower figure of 66½ million.

To such observers the fall in fertility rates must appear dramatic: considered with a wider perspective however, the seemingly dramatic change in birth rate after 1964 may be considered none other than a return to the long term trend begun in 1880, from which the increase in birth rate during the world war and subsequently between 1955 and 1964 were short term fluctuations, of the type likely to occur during periods of social transition.

Demographers describe this long term drop in fertility in developed countries by a mix of conditions called 'modernization'. This condition is likely to occur whenever a society becomes industrialized, educated and urban, for in these conditions, natural determination towards large families – the need for children to till the land, the need to produce a dozen children for fear that few if any will survive – is insignificant alongside the economic costs of producing children – the cost of schooling and further education and the increasing standard of living which children expect almost as a right.

The re-assertion of this long term trend, through which America and the other countries of the European Continent are also passing, has been caused by just such basic socio-economic factors. There has been a marked tendency to defer births in the early years of marriage, a tendency increasingly helped by better and more knowledgeable use of birth control. The Equal Pay Act and the Equal Opportunities Acts of the early 1970s have increased women's awareness of career opportunities and the economic and social advantages of delaying their family. At the same time, inflation, higher unemployment and what a French population expert has called 'the economic and social anxiety that haunts us all' have furthered an awareness of the costs of having children.

CHAPTER 4
THE CHANGING STRUCTURE
OF POPULATION

The changing structure of population
Changes in the structure of population are no less important than changes in total size, for they too produce social and economic consequences.

The most important composite changes that occur are changes in age structure and changes in sex distribution.

Age distribution
As population increase occurs, changes in the relative importance of different age groups within the total take place.

A population with a stable birth rate and death rate can be illustrated by sex/age distribution pyramid. The pyramid shows that in the higher age groups each group has fewer members than the last,

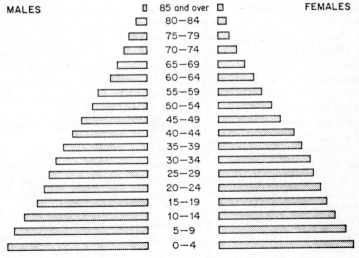

MALES			FEMALES

85 and over
80—84
75—79
70—74
65—69
60—64
55—59
50—54
45—49
40—44
35—39
30—34
25—29
20—24
15—19
10—14
5—9
0—4

Fig. 10. *Stable population age pyramid (high birth- and death-rates)*

the pyramid moving to its apex as the death rate in the higher age groups increase and the expectation of life decreases.

If the younger age groups increase more than proportionately to the higher age groups, a beehive result will occur, as was the case in the United Kingdom around 1891. This beehive effect in the age structure of population occurred because of the marked fall in the death rate during the nineteenth century, accompanied by a generally high birth rate. This 'beehive' effect is illustrated below in Figure 9:

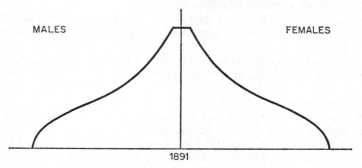

Fig. 11. *British Population Age Pyramid 1891*

The Royal Commission on Population which was published in 1949 produced another pyramid for the population around 1947. It is a strange looking pyramid, bulging in the middle age groups, but it effectively illustrates the rising average age of the population occasioned by the falling birth rate after 1911, coupled with a continuing decline in death rates and accompanying increase in the expectation of life. The small increase in the 0–4 age groups is due to the expansion of the birth rate at the end of the war.

By the end of the century the normal pyramid shape is likely to re-assert itself.

Changes in the age structure of population have important economic and social implications. The most important implication is the relationship between the working and the non-working population. This is the dependency ratio, or, as it is sometimes called – the burden of dependents. The larger the dependent groups, the greater is the burden on the working population from whose production and resultant incomes, resources have to be found to support their dependents.

The working population is normally taken to be those men and

48

women who pay national insurance, between the ages of 15–65 and are registered as willing to work. Thus the dependent age groups are the children and young people between 0–15 years, the minimum age for school leaving, and the older men and women over the age of 65.

Obviously, there are many exceptions to this arbitrary division.

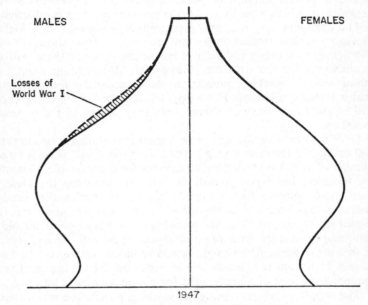

Fig. 12. *British Population Age Pyramid 1947*

There are many students in full-time education and thus dependent on their parents and the state, who are well over the age of 15 (the average University student does not enter full-time employment until the age of 22). Similarly there are many older men and women who continue in full and part-time employment well after the age of 65. These two age groups tend to cancel each other out statistically, so that it is reasonable to regard the age groups 15–65 as the economically active part of the population.

If the average age of the population is becoming younger, the tendency will be for the dependency ratio to become lower. The burden on the working population will decrease meaning that relatively smaller amounts of money will have to be paid out by the public services in pension funds, hospital services, old-age homes, etc. If the average age of the population is increasing it means that the dependency ratio is increasing and the burden on the working population is increasing too. This would mean that a proportionately smaller working population would have to find the resources to finance a greater amount of public services for the benefits of the dependents, which would increase the pressure on their productivity.

The changing age structure, giving either a younger or a higher average age has further important economic implications. If the average age of the population is becoming younger there will be implications for the structure of aggregate demand, the supply of labour into the working population, the composition and quality of that working population. If the population is becoming older, there will be the same range of effects, only they will be in the opposite direction.

With a lower average age the composition of aggregate demand will reflect the tastes of young people. This trend will affect a larger number of industries traditionally catering for older people. Consider for instance, the rapid growth of industry supplying the teenage market, the market for teenage fashions, the market for teenage clothes, magazines and newspapers, leisure activities and even the consumer durable market, which traditionally has supplied the older age group. Consider the enormous impact of advertising and styling in interior designs, furnishings, cars, and ladies' fashions. The fast-back GT concept is one example in cars, and the raising (and subsequent lowering) of skirt lengths for all age groups is another.

The supply of labour joining the working population will increase in time. Increasing numbers of young people in the 0–15 age groups will mean that this 'bulge' will eventually enter the working population. The size of the working population will increase and also its average age will be younger. A lower average age means that it is likely that the attitudes towards occupational training will be more flexible and adaptable to change, in all fields. Changing structures of industry, new technology and innovations, new job styles, new demands will all be more easily met with a younger rather than older working population, purely on the grounds that the young are more flexible than the old.

There will be greater mobility of labour of all kinds, both occupational, and geographical. The young are more ready to change occupations and even industries, if they feel that they need to 'get ahead' and geographical location will not stand in their way. Thus it is likely that both internal and external migration will increase with a younger working population, both willing and able to move around, in their search for the right occupation.

In some ways the post-war bulge in the birth rate has already affected the market. Perambulators, infants' shoes and baby food were in high demand in 1948 and 1949, and more recently the sales of toys has risen. The potential demand for 'pop' records is already rapidly rising as the babies of 1946–48 enter their second stage of rocking. But the really important effects are yet to come; for these will be due to the forthcoming increase in available juvenile labour and the not far away boom in marriages . . . teenagers accounted for 'at least 25 per cent of all consumer expenditure on bicycles and motor cycles, on records and record players, on cosmetics and toilet preparations, and on cinema and other forms of entertainment.' They were important also for such things as confectionery, and soft drinks, clothing and footwear, sports goods, magazines and cigarettes.[1]

With an ageing population the effects will affect similar areas of the economy but they will be in the opposite direction. Thus, the changing composition of aggregate demand will be towards those goods and services demanded by the middle and older age groups, the working population will both contract and have a higher average, making it less adaptable, less able to adjust to innovation and technological change, and it will certainly be less mobile both geographically and occupationally.

Britain experienced an ageing population up to the Second World War but, because of two periods of population increases, it appeared unlikely that this would be so from the mid-sixties through to the end of the century. Between 1911–69, $13\frac{1}{2}$ million people were added to the population of the country. By 1971 they were predominantly in the middle age groups, but the 11 million it was then thought would be added to the population, between 1971 and the end of the century, would be in younger age groups, ensuring that the average age of the UK population would drop to the year 2000.

Average age of U.K. population

	1965	1970	1980	1990	2000
Males	34·2	33·9	33·2	32·5	31·7
Females	37·5	37·1	36·2	35·2	34·0

[1] J. Parry Lewis, 'Young People and the Pattern of the Economy', *Lloyds Bank Review*, July 1961.

While the birth rate was increasing it was likely that the dependency ratio would increase too. 1971 figures suggested that a dependency ratio which had been 606 in 1911 and 655 in 1969 would increase to 675 in 1990, figures which, expressed as a percentage of total population, show a rise from 38·2 per cent in 1965 to a peak of 42·9 per cent in 1990.

Recent changes in birth rate, and a slowing to zero population growth, have affected both the projected dependency ratio and the average age of population. The dependency ratio is now expected to fall from its present figure of 33 per cent to a figure in the year 2000 of 39 per cent. At the same time the average age of the population is likely to rise assuming that present trends continue, as is assumed by the official 1976 projections.

In theory, a lowering of the average age of population and a lowering of the dependency ratio suggests a lessening of the burden on the working population and the economy. It seems possible that the theoretical fall in the working population, made likely by falling birth rates, will be more than offset by an increase in the numbers of women entering and remaining within this section of the population, a tendency made possible by changing attitudes to women's role within society, legislation of the 1970s and a greater acceptance of a woman's responsibility as a second breadwinner. However, any decrease in demand for social services arising from smaller numbers is likely to be offset by increasing demand for higher standards in all social services.

Sex distribution

The distribution of the sexes is fundamental to the structure of population in a country. The 'normal' sex distribution, or ratio of men to women at birth is 105:100. On the other hand the life expectancy of males has always been lower.

Given these two factors, it is expected that there will be a small excess of males over females through all the age groups up to late middle age. In Britain the normal male excess is expected to be very small up to the age of fifty, after which females will predominate.

But in fact a more normal state of the sex ratio for the United Kingdom during most of the last hundred years has been an excess of females, through the reproductive age range from 15–49. The table below illustrates this well.

Sex Ratio – in the age group 15–49 in U.K.

1851	107 females to 100 males
1891	109
1911	108
1921	113
1931	110
1939	106
1947	102

(*Royal Commission on Population*, 1949)

This unnatural excess of female to males in age groups which theoretically should show an excess of males has been caused, during the nineteenth century by the net loss from migration and the large number of men, who saw service in the overseas colonies. World War One had the effect of wiping out a large proportion of the male population between the ages of 17–30. This had a marked effect on the sex ratio in 1921, when it became 113 females to every 100 males, and this can be said to have affected the total size and the age structure of the British population to the present day.

The most important trend in Britain with regard to the sex ratio is the general raising of the age level when males cease to outnumber females. This barrier has been raised from 25 in 1931, to 35 in 1961, to 45 in 1971, and it is projected that before the end of the century this level will have been raised to 60, all the result of decreasing male infant and child mortality.

The geographical distribution of the sexes might be assumed to be equal. It would seem logical that wherever men are, there will be women too! In fact, this is not so. There is an excess of women over men in urban areas, particularly in the conurbations, and in coastal resorts, where elderly people tend to retire. This imbalance represents wider job opportunities for female employment in the towns and a greater variety of social amenities, catering as much for women as for men. It is also explained by perhaps the most significant trend concerning the sex distribution in the United Kingdom, that of the great excess of females to males in the older age groups. The present estimate is that at the age of eighty there will be two women for every man, and at the age of eighty-five, almost three women for every man.

The distribution of the sexes is important for any demographic analysis. A severe imbalance of the sex ratio will seriously change the flow of population, both now and in the future – to say nothing of the happiness of the men and women concerned! Changes in the ratio will affect growth projections, family size, average age of

53

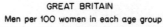

GREAT BRITAIN
Men per 100 women in each age group

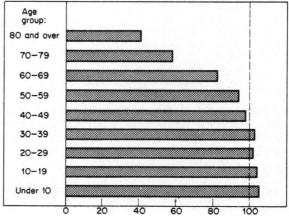

marriage, birth rates, and the patterns of aggregate demand within the economy.

Occupational distribution

An important population distribution in any country is that of the working population or occupational distribution. Linked closely as it is to age and sex structure, and thus to the dependency ratio, it is a critical factor determining to some extent the productive potential of an economy. Changes in total size and in the relative size of industrial groups within the working population give clues as to the changing structure of the economy as well as to the growing labour potential.

CHAPTER 5
EXTERNAL AND
INTERNAL MIGRATION

The history of the world is the history of migration. Carlo Cippolla in his *Economic History of World Population* has drawn attention to the migrations which have affected the spread of the agricultural revolution from the Near East to all parts of Europe. President Kennedy called America 'A Nation of Immigrants' and the United Kingdom is itself a country peopled by immigrants initially from all over Europe and now from much further afield.

Recently migration has become of special importance to Britain. During the 1950s increasing numbers of Commonwealth citizens came to live in Britain, the inflow reaching greatest proportions in the later years of the decade. This made for special problems in certain areas and new legislation to control the flow.

At the same time, a number of highly qualified personnel left this country to work abroad, particularly in the United States and Canada, because they felt that their skills and talents would be rewarded better in those countries than in Britain. This outflow came to be known as 'the Brain Drain'. It too reached worrying proportions, because it was obvious that the type of persons emigrating were the persons required by the domestic economy to help revitalize investment and management.

Internal migration became increasingly important also. From the beginnings of the Industrial Revolution to the present day internal migration has taken place; there has been a general movement of people away from the land into the industrialized urban areas. This movement was still taking place with a renewed vigour towards the South East region with its magnet of London. This has created an imbalance of resources in the home economy and has produced special problems of high density living and overpopulation in some areas whilst in others, the problems are similar to those of the developing regions overseas.

External migration
Migration can drastically affect the age and sex distribution of the

55

population, as well as the total size. Typically, migrants have been young, male, and unmarried. This is because men are generally more adventurous than women or because older people, having fewer family ties or responsibilities, find it easier to travel longer distances and have more job opportunities, with prospects of higher earnings.

This has been the traditional pattern of external migration through history and it is still true today from countries such as Yugoslavia, Greece and Italy, and from the developing countries of the world. However, recently female migrants have come to play a more important role: there are more female migrants out of the United Kingdom than ever before. This is due to the greater freedom that women have gained during this century, the improving job and earning opportunities open to women and the improved freedom of movement accorded to women socially.

The reasons behind migration are many and various. Basically, it is possible to distinguish two different types of migration – voluntary and involuntary.

Economic reasons are the major causes of voluntary migration. Improved job or career opportunities are important in persuading both skilled and unskilled labour to move across national boundaries. There may, as in the case of Ireland at present, be a severe shortage of job opportunities at home, while the shortage of labour in another country may provide just the outlet that an individual needs to pull him to make the decision. Similarly, the prospects of better career opportunities and superior equipment and environment has played an important role in persuading qualified personnel from the United Kingdom to leave careers in scientific research and medicine at home, to migrate to America and Canada.

Involuntary or 'forced' migration is caused by pressures outside the control of the individuals. Historically political and religious persecution has played an important role in persuading people to move. The United States of America was originally peopled by persons responding to this motivation and since then, America has gathered large inflows of peoples from Europe as a result of all the traditional pressures such as war, starvation and famine, transportation, and other political decisions.

A study by D. J. Bogue identified three basic elements in migration.[1] These were:

---

[1] D. J. Bogue, *Internal Migration in the Study of Population*, edited by P. M. Hansen & C. D. Duncan, Chicago University Press, 1959.

1. Migration stimulating condition.
2. Factors in choosing destination.
3. Socio-economic conditions affecting migration.

Under these general headings came a whole host of different factors.

1. Education – lack of marriages – marriage – employment offers – opportunities or bonanzas – gold rushes – migratory work – special skills – transfer of employment – sale of business – loss of a farm – discharge from employment – low wages – retirement – death of a relative – military service – medical care – imprisonment – political, religious, social persecution or oppression – natural disasters – invasion by outsiders – inheritance – wanderlust – maladjustment to the community – social rejection – forced movement – population pressure and growth – climate – availability of land – war.

2. Cost of moving – distance – presence of relatives – friends – employment offer – physical attractiveness of community – physical environment – population composition – amenities – cultural similarities – availability of land – special employment facilities – familiarity of knowledge – special assistance of subsidies – information – reputation – lack of alternative destinations – climate – transportation facilities.

3. Major capital investment – major business recessions or fluctuations – technological change – changes in economic organization – provisions for social welfare – migration for propaganda purposes – regulations affecting migration – living conditions and levels – tolerance of minorities – migration policy – wars.

The nineteenth century and the period up to World War Two were periods when Britain 'exported' a large number of people. It is estimated that upwards of twenty million people emigrated to destinations outside Europe between the beginning of the nineteenth century, and the 1930s. At the same time large numbers of Europeans and Empire citizens emigrated to Britain, which tended to offset this large figure, but the new flow was still outward. In the period 1871–1931 a net outflow of four million persons resulted.

Net Gain or Loss from Migration

1871–81	−257,000	1958	+ 45,000	1966	−95,000
1881–91	−817,000	1959	+ 44,000	1968	−68,000
1891–1901	−122,000	1960	+ 82,000	1970	−39,000
1901–11	−756,000	1961	+170,000	1972	− 5000
1911–21	−858,000	1962	+136,000	1973	−72,000
1921–31	−565,000	1963	+ 10,000	1974	−67,000
1931–41	−650,000	1964	− 60,000	1975	−29,000

See also p. 62, para. 2.

After twenty years of being a net immigrant country, emigration from the UK has become important again. In the build up to the 1964 General Election, the then leader of the Opposition, Mr. Harold Wilson repeatedly drew attention to the problem of what came to be called 'the Brain Drain' and identified its causes as the deficiencies of the British industrial system, or of the British Government's management of research and technology, in that it did not give the status, the prospects, and the dignity, and the opportunities that these highly trained scientists and technologists should have.[1]

These words are presented more starkly and with greater impact by the statistics of the Ministry of Technology. The table below draws attention to the fact that 19 per cent of the 1963 output of newly qualified doctors and technologists, and 9 per cent of that of scientists were lost to the economy of this country. This figure represents a new loss to the economy, for our emigrants were not being replaced by immigrants of similar skill or training.

Estimated emigration of British and Commonwealth engineers, technologists and scientists going abroad for a minimum of one year (compared with new supply 1958 to 1963)

(*Figures rounded to the nearest hundred*)

Date	Total emigration of suitable Engineers and technologists	Total	Engineers and technologists as percentage of new supply three years earlier	Total	Scientists as percentage of new supply three years earlier
1961	3200	1900	24	1300	22
1962	3500	2200	27	1300	20
1963	4000	2500	27	1500	20
1964	4700	3100	32	1700	22
1965	5100	3300	36	1800	22
1966	6200	4200	42	2000	23

(Ministry of Technology.)

Notes:
1. By international definition, an emigrant is one who intends to remain abroad for at least a year. A proportion of those classed as emigrants by this definition later return to their home country.
2. Most of these emigrants are 'British' rather than 'Commonwealth' and they have generally had at least two or three years' further educa-

---

[1] H. Wilson, Speech at the Usher Hall, Edinburgh, March 21st, 1964.

tion, training or experience since their first degree or professional qualification.

3. The comparison of outflow with the new supply three years earlier is arbitrary, but it is based on the assumption that on average these emigrants will have qualified about three years before they leave the U.K.

The importance of this development is the changed nature of the emigrants. Emigration from Britain has always been a fact, but recently, the highly selective nature of the emigrants coupled with the acknowledged shortage of the self-same qualified personnel at home has produced a dangerous situation. Not only is their potential skill and enterprise removed from the economy, but the home economy which they are leaving has already borne the cost of their training and general education. In effect, the cost to the economy is doubled.

Human capital has long been recognized by economists and businessmen to be the most valuable form of capital. In order to find remedies it is important to understand the reasons for this outflow of skilled personnel. From surveys and questionnaires conducted with emigrants to North America the following general forces have been given:

1. Better equipped educational centres, with high reputations, for research.
2. The image of North America as a young man's country. The belief that there are fewer barriers to promotion or social movement in the States compared with England.
3. Salary – in real and money terms salaries are higher in North America than they are in Britain particularly in the growth technological industries.
4. Capital is easier to accumulate; taxation levels, and in particular marginal rates of taxation are lower than in the United Kingdom.
5. There are greater fringe benefits such as share ownership and options, which are more liberally treated in the U.S.A. than in the U.K. for tax purposes.
6. The social status of the engineer, technocrat and professional man is higher in North America than it is in Britain.

Immigration

Immigration must be accounted the most dramatic and potentially the most explosive issue in recent British political life. For this reason, it is important to put immigration into Britain into its proper perspective.

From the map above it is immediately obvious that the origins of the British nation are very mixed. Taking the migrations up to 1066, the basic pattern of what is now called Anglo-Saxon Britain was established. The original settlers were the Old Stone Age peoples who migrated into England across the land bridge from Europe. They are known to have inhabited the region of the Thames Valley, the Devon and Welsh coasts and the region along the Severn Valley. The oldest descendants of this group are still living in Central Wales. The last major settlement, the Normans, under William the Conqueror came in 1066. Although not the majority of the population the Normans were conquerors who imposed their law and culture on Britain.

Immigration did not stop with the Normans. Since 1066 there have been many additions to our ethnic groups. But large though they appeared at the time, they were all minority migrations bringing a group into a population which was prepared to absorb and integrate with them in time. In the sixteenth and seventeenth centuries came the big Dutch and Flemish inflows, resulting from the persecution of Protestants by Spain. The settlers did much to revitalize the weaving industry so important to the early English economy. In 1685, 40,000 Huguenots fled to England from France to escape Louis XIV's persecution, following the Revocation of the Edict of Nantes and they too contributed to the economy; the woollen and cotton spinning industry benefited enormously, and it was a descendant of the Huguenots, Thomas Lombe, who erected the first textile factory in England at Derby in 1711. A lifting of the immigration laws by Cromwell, allowed for an inflow of Jewish migrants from Portugal, Spain and the Spanish Netherlands. The development of the basic industries during the Industrial Revolution brought many Germans to Yorkshire. The nineteenth century also saw a massive inflow of Irish immigrants which has continued to this day; in one week in 1847, Liverpool took 130,000 Irish immigrants. In this century, important minority inflows have been the 250,000 Central European migrants who fled from the Nazi persecution during the 1930s, the Ashkenazi Jews, who came to Britain to escape pogroms in Russia, Poland, Lithuania in the years before the First World War and more recently the big inflows from the Commonwealth. As Ronald Bryden said 'in this nation of immigrants, the turbaned Sikh conductor on the Bradford bus is just as much a John Bull as the Normans, Danes, Jutes,

EARLY BRITISH IMMIGRANT SETTLERS: STONE AGE to 1066

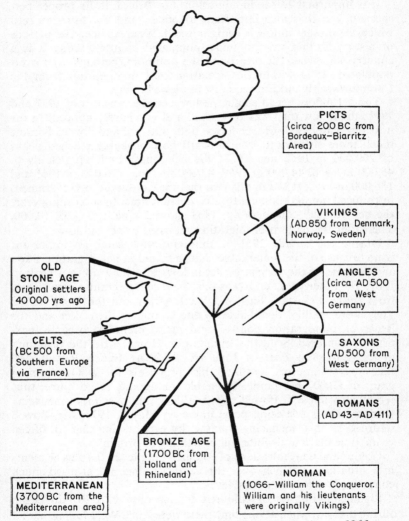

PICTS
(circa 200 BC from
Bordeaux-Biarritz
Area)

VIKINGS
(AD 850 from Denmark,
Norway, Sweden)

**OLD
STONE AGE**
Original settlers
40 000 yrs ago

ANGLES
(circa AD 500
from West
Germany

CELTS
(BC 500 from
Southern Europe
via France)

SAXONS
(AD 500 from
West Germany)

ROMANS
(AD 43—AD 411)

BRONZE AGE
(1700 BC from
Holland and
Rhineland)

NORMAN
(1066—William the Conqueror.
William and his lieutenants
were originally Vikings)

MEDITERRANEAN
(3700 BC from the
Mediterranean area)

Fig. 13. *Early British Immigrant Settlers: Stone Age to 1066*

Angles, Celts and Stone Age Iberians who made their way to these shores centuries ago.'[1]

It is important to see immigration into Britain in its proper perspective, but it is also important to understand the situation into which the present inflow is being injected. Whereas in earlier periods of history Britain was an under-populated country, today it is a country somewhere at or around the optimum, perhaps even over-populated. It is within this situation that immigration from the Commonwealth and Europe must be viewed today.

The net inflow began sometime between the censuses of 1931 and 1951; the inflow then was very small and was hardly noticed. In the next ten years, 1951–61, the flows, both outward and inward became much more significant. The outward flow probably reached peaks of 200,000 in 1952 and 1957; the *net* inflow built up steadily to 45,000 in 1958, 44,000 in 1959, 82,000 in 1960, 170,000 in 1961 and 136,000 in 1962. It was in this year that the Conservative Government introduced immigration control for the first time. In succeeding years the net flow fell considerably; 1963 showed a net inflow of 10,000. Thereafter the pattern of migration returned to net outflows.

During the decade 1951–61 immigration became an important issue because of the remarkable change round in net migration flows and because of the very large net inflows that built up to a peak in 1961. The other vital factor was that the recent migrants came largely from India, Pakistan, East and West Africa and the West Indies. They were readily identifiable by the colour of their skin and the issues of immigration control and racial prejudice became inextricably confused.'Send the Immigrants Home' read the headlines in the *Yorkshire Post* of June 10, 1970, as Enoch Powell MP for Wolverhampton, outlined his proposals for a Government grant of £2,000 per family to enable immigrants to go home, thus removing what Mr. Powell called 'a dark and ever more menacing shadow.' On a television programme on May 2, 1971, Mr. Powell returned to this 'menacing shadow' by prophesying that 'In fifteen years' time black and white will be fighting in Britain'.

Colour and concentrations of coloured people are the new elements in a situation in which over the centuries, has not aroused much controversy except on a local level.

Significant inflows of coloured immigration into Britain began during the war, when at one time there were 7,000 West Indians alone

---

[1] *The Observer*, February 1, 1967.

Net migrants beyond the British Isles

| | United Kingdom | | | | | | | Thousands |
| | Mid-year to mid-year | | | | | | | |
	1964 –65	1966 –67	1968 –69	1970 –71	1972 –73	1973 –74	1974 –75	1975 –76
Citizenship*								
Aliens	+22	+30	+21	+21	+24	+23	+20	+15
Old Commonwealth	+ 1	+ 5	– 2	– 5	+ 3	+ 6	0	+ 3
New Commonwealth	+55	+45	+48	+33	+11	+11	+17	+20
United Kingdom citizens	–136	–175	–136	–88	–42	–112	–104	–67
of which								
UK passport holders from East Africa	—	—	+ 8	+ 9	+34	+10	+13	+12
All migrants beyond the British Isles†	–58	–95	–68	–39	– 5	–72	–67	–29
of which: inflow	223	231	228	227	225	183	194	191
outflow	281	326	296	266	230	255	261	220

Source: Office of Population Censuses and Surveys

* Pakistani citizens are included in 'New Commonwealth' up to and including 1971–72, but in 'Aliens' in 1972–73 and thereafter.

† Excluding net immigration due to direct traffic with the Irish Republic which may have averaged some 10,000 persons per annum during the 1961–71 intercensal period.

serving in the RAF. The majority of these people returned home after the war, but finding economic and social conditions at a lower standard, a significant number might have been persuaded to retrace their steps to Britain. Certainly, many provided a living advertisement for the good life and improving job opportunities in Britain. As early as 1948 an inflow of West Indian immigrants began to arrive, and after the 1952 McCarran-Walter immigration control act in the USA, which limited migration to the States to 100 Jamaicans per year, the flows increased to significant numbers. The period 1952–62 showed very significant increases in the number of immigrants from the West Indies. It is important and interesting to notice that the inflows were not steady but responded to fluctuations in the demand for labour. Figure 14 illustrates this point.

It is important to realize that active immigration was encouraged by organizations such as the Barbadian Immigrants Liason Service by arranging jobs with the London Transport Executive (from 1956) and the British Hotels and Restaurants Association.[1]

Indian and Pakistani immigration did not really begin until the 1950s. As with the West Indian immigration, the general tendency was for increasing numbers to come to live in this country, but unlike West Indian immigration the flow was not affected by changing demand for labour and some two-thirds of the Pakistan–Indian immigrant flow has come into Britain since immigration control was enforced.

There are other differences too. Whereas the West Indian immigration was characterized by a very high proportion of women, the Indian-Pakistani inflow contained an overwhelmingly high proportion of men. A survey in Southall in 1950 revealed that the estimated proportion of women was as low as 4 per cent in the Sikh community; in Bradford the 1961 Census revealed 3,376 men and only eighty-one women. However since 1962, this pattern has tended to change a little, as more Pakistanis have brought over their wives and families. But in general West Indians tended to be family settlers, whilst Pakistanis have tended to be employment immigrants.

The typical characteristics of coloured immigrants are, that they are more likely to be male, that they are usually young adults, that they live in a greater state of overcrowding than their English counter-

---

[1] Nicholas Deakin, *Colour, Citizenship and British Society*, Panther, 1970.

parts, and they tend to congregate in urban areas, particularly in Greater London and the West Midlands.

The great disparity between the sexes is illustrated by the table below. It also reveals the important difference in sex ratio between

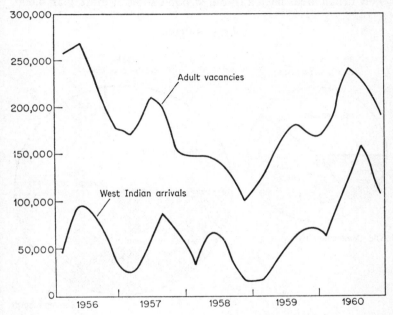

Fig. 14. *Quarterly figures of West Indian Arrivals and Employment Vacancies*
(G. C. K. Peach, *West Indian Migration to Britain*)

different racial groups, which obviously leads to different social problems, once the men and women have settled in their new country.

Historically it is the young who migrate. Commonwealth immigration to Britain is no exception. The vast majority of immigrants are under the age of thirty. Because of children born to immigrants the average age of the black population actually fell between 1961–66. The table below illustrates age structure in the Greater London and West Midlands conurbations in 1966.

The 1966 10 per cent sample survey showed that immigrants tend to live in more overcrowded conditions than a comparable English family. If we take a density of one-and-a-half persons per room, only 2·6 per cent of households in England and Wales lived at or above this density in 1961. The figure for all immigrant households was 9·6 per cent and for Caribbean households was 37·3 per cent.

Few urban areas have a coloured population of more than 4,000.

UNITED KINGDOM

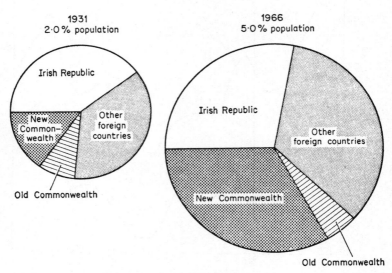

Fig. 15. *People Born Overseas*

Those that have are in the Greater London area or in the West Midlands, although Nottingham has perhaps 12,000 West Indians, Bradford some 12,000 Pakistanis, Manchester and Liverpool 10,000 coloured immigrants and Leeds, Coventry, Huddersfield, Bristol, Leicester and Sheffield between 6–7,000 each. At local authority level London has the greatest concentration; in 1966 there were only six boroughs in the whole country with greater than 5 per cent coloured population and all of these were in the Greater London area: the boroughs of Brent 7·4 per cent, Hackney 7·1 per cent, Lambeth 6·7 per cent, Haringey 5·6 per cent, Islington 5·4 per cent and Hammersmith 5·4 per cent. The table on page 68 outlines the national distribution of coloured population.

Number of Males per 1,000 Females among Immigrants, 1961 and 1966

Area of origin	England and Wales			London conurbation 1966	West Midland conurbation 1966	West Yorks conurbation 1966
	At 1961	Arrivals 1961–66	At 1966			
India*	1,568	1,373	1,479	1,520	1,644	1,640
Pakistan*	5,380	3,451	4,231	2,890	9,451	5,394
Jamaica	1,258	773	1,066	983	1,181	1,356
Rest of Caribbean	1,264	809	1,026	1,048	1,152	1,145
British W. Africa	1,949	1,452	1,614	1,572	—	—
All coloured	1,548	1,279	1,394	1,230	1,754	4,418
Cyprus	1,273	1,016	1,191	1,182	1,484	—
Total Population	937	—	940	916	979	949

* Excluding white Indians and Pakistanis.
(*Colour and Citizenship.*)

Both the total and the proportion of coloured people in the British population has been increasing. In 1951 it was estimated that there were only 75,000 coloured persons who had been born in Britain. In 1961 the total had risen to 882,000 and in 1966 it had increased further to 924,000. Proportionately these totals represent in 1951 1·7 persons per 1,000 of population and 7·3 persons in 1961. In 1961 the total had

Comparative Age Structure of Different Immigrant Groups at the 1966 Census, Greater London and West Midlands Conurbations

Age (years)	*India	Pakistan	Jamaica	Rest of Caribbean	British W. Africa	Cyprus	Total pop.
0–14	33%	24%	40%	39%	23%	35%	23%
15–24	16%	15%	11%	12%	16%	18%	14%
24–44	40%	51%	41%	41%	59%	34%	25%
45+	11%	10%	8%	8%	2%	13%	38%

* Excluding white Indians.
1966 Census.

risen to 882,000, in 1966 to 924,000 and in 1971 it had increased to 1,151,000.

Within the groups of immigrants Jamaicans form the largest single group with 30 per cent of the coloured population, whilst the West Indians, with 49 per cent are the most important general racial groups of all. The table on page 69 shows the growth of an immigrant population as a proportion of total United Kingdom population and the relative importance of the different ethnic groups.

The publicity surrounding the growth of coloured immigration has tended to obscure another very important migrant trend – that of Irish immigration. Irish immigration has continued constantly since the potato famine of 1846–48. This outward movement was to both the United States and the United Kingdom, but since the First World War it has been chiefly to the United Kingdom.

The figures in the table on page 70 give some idea of the scale of this migration. The consequences to the Irish economy and Irish society have varied depending on the net effect on particular regions. The range of depopulation between the years 1926–1951 varies from 29·1 to 1 per cent. During this period only fourteen out of the

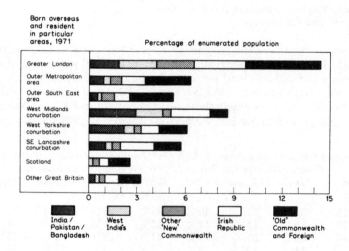

thirty-seven Irish Republic and Northern Ireland provinces experienced an *increase* of population.

English people of the nineteenth century were well aware of the influx of Irishmen, particularly if they lived in towns such as Liverpool, or near a major piece of engineering work such as the railways. This inflow continued through the nineteenth century and increased in pace after the First World War. Through the 1950s England and Wales received around 45,000 a year net gain from Northern Ireland, the Irish Republic and from Scotland. In the period 1961–64

England experienced a net gain of 31,000 per annum from the Irish Republic and another 30,000 from Northern Ireland and Scotland combined.

People Born Overseas
United Kingdom

Birthplace	1931	1951	1961	1966	1971
Number of people (thousands):					
Foreign countries	347	722	842	886	980
'Old' Commonwealth	75	99	110	125	143
'New' Commonwealth	137	218	541	853	1,151
Republic of Ireland	362	532	709	732	709
Total born overseas	921	1,571	2,202	2,596	2,983
As percentage of population:					
Foreign countries	0·6	1·5	1·6	1·7	1·8
'Old' Commonwealth	0·2	0·2	0·2	0·2	0·3
'New' Commonwealth	0·3	0·4	1·1	1·6	2·1
Republic of Ireland	0·8	1·1	1·4	1·4	1·3
Total born overseas	2·0	3·2	4·3	5·0	5·5

The effects of large scale immigration on the United Kingdom's economy are important. They can be divided into economic effects and social effects.

The economic effects concern in particular the changes in aggregate demand and their effect on their general equilibrium of the economy, and the changing distribution of income. E. J. Mishan and L. Needleman[1] have spent some considerable time erecting models to quantify such effects and have come up with conclusions that support a much lower rate of immigration. They postulate that the British population is very near – or possibly over – the optimum, so that any net immigration is going to add to the problem (for an understanding of this concept refer back to diagram on p. 17). This being so the economic effects will follow the theory. The effects on income per head of a rate of inflow of half a million immigrants will only be small. But in the case of distribution of income the effect will be much greater – in all cases wages fall in relation to profits.

Again, if the economy of the country is at or near the full employment equilibrium position the effect of an inflow of immigrant labour

---

[1] *Lloyds Bank Review*, July 1966.

Population at each Census since 1891 (Ireland)

Year	Total population	Inter-censal period	Births regis-tered	Deaths regis-tered	Natural increase (births minus deaths)	De-crease popula-tion	Esti-mated net Emigra-tion
					(in period mentioned in third column)		
1891	3,468,694	1881–1891	835,072	639,073	195,999	401,326	597,325
1901	3,221,823	1891–1901	737,934	588,391	149,543	246,871	396,414
1911	3,139,688	1901–1911	713,709	534,305	179,404	82,135	261,539
1926	2,971,992	1911–1926	968,742	731,409	237,333	167,696	405,029
1936	2,968,420	1926–1936	583,502	420,323	163,179	3,572	166,751
1946	2,955,107	1936–1946	602,095	428,297	173,798	13,313	187,111
1951	2,960,593	1946–1951	322,335	197,281	125,054	+5,486	119,568
1956	2,898,264	1951–1956	312,517	178,083	134,434	62,329	196,763
1961	2,818,341	1956–1961	302,816	170,736	132,080	79,923	212,003
1966	2,880,752	1961–1966	312,709	166,443	146,266	+62,411	83,855

R. K. Kelsall, *Population.*

will be damaging. Increasing the labour supply will create problems of public finance and budgeting, unemployment and inflationary pressures. Mishan and Needleman argue that the cause of the so-called labour shortage in Britain during the Sixties was caused by mismanagement of the economy, leading to excessive demand for goods and thereby creating a shortage of labour. This labour shortage has been general, applying to both skilled and unskilled labour, and inflows of immigrants have eased the pressure on resources at the unskilled – and in some cases the skilled – end of the labour market.

The 'essential' services argument is important. It can be argued that 'life would be harder for us without coloured labour'. The special correspondent of *The Times* wrote in 1966:

In many mills (in Bradford) the night shift is composed almost entirely of Pakistanis. Apart from the administrative and clerical staff, 20 per cent of the male textile force in the locality are coloured. Britain could not live as she does without her coloured immigrants. The health service would break down; roughly 40 per cent of the doctors of British hospitals up to consultant level come from overseas; the greater part from India and Pakistan; about 17 per cent of the trainee nurses alone in England and Wales come from the Commonwealth, and about half of them are in the four Metropolitan regions. London Transport would be severely disrupted; over 3,000 Barbadians alone have been brought over under schemes to London. Bus services in several of our major cities would suffer badly. Important sections of industry in the

Midlands would slow down. The shortage of bricks would worsen. Lunches would be harder to get in London cafes; streets in some cities would become filthy. Life in Britain for many people who criticize coloured immigrants most would be harder and more unpleasant without them.

If this argument appears conclusive, Mishan and Needleman sound a note of caution. They suggest that if immigrant labour had not been available the service might have been reduced in quality or become more expensive (consistent with the elementary laws of supply and demand), but equally labour-saving devices might have been produced to solve the problem which would have been to the long term advantage of the population, not least for those workers engaged in the trades and professions which were supplied with immigrant workers, whose wages might have been raised as a result of the shortage.

Inflows of immigrants will affect not only the total population, but the age and sex structure of the population as well, with consequent effects on the future size of the population. We have seen already that immigrants are predominantly male and young, being under the age of thirty. Both these factors will have some effect on projections of future population.

Taking 1966 as a base-line, Valerie Jackson has estimated that the 1968 immigrant population would increase to 1,113,000 and the projection to 1969 would be, 1,185,000. Projections were based on the birth and death rates plus the effects of any new entrants into the country. Death rates are likely to be similar to indigenous population rates, but it seems likely that birth rates will be higher. The number of children born to West Indian families is particularly large. The Registrar General's Report for 1965 put West Indian families at the top of the list for family size, 73 per cent above the national average; Irish Republic families were 35 per cent above, Northern Irish families 22 per cent above and Indian and Pakistan families 14 per cent above. Attempts at a prediction of certain parts of the total population are likely to be very inaccurate. Thus Miss Jackson has suggested high and low fertility projections in her study. On a low fertility growth rate estimated coloured population in 1986 would be 2,074,000 and on a high fertility estimate the number would be 2,373,000. On balance it seems likely that immigrant families will maintain a higher than average fertility but that it is likely for this trend to diminish the longer immigrants remain in the country.

Since Valerie Jackson's studies the 1971 Census and more recent population statistics have suggested a changing trend. The 1973 statistics show that the number of births in this country to women born in East and West Africa, India, Pakistan, Bangladesh, Malta, Gibraltar and Cyprus declined from 46,100 between April 1969 and March 1970 to 43,000 in 1973. The Registrar-General's figures show that the birth rate among mothers from the new Commonwealth was down by 7 per cent in 1973 compared with 1969; whilst Asian mothers were constant in their births, West Indian mothers, previously at the top of the birth rate tables, had 28 per cent fewer children in 1973 than in 1969.

The social effects are difficult to quantify and are notoriously open to subjective evaluation. The fact is that the different colour of the newer immigrants emphasizes the difference in their customs, attitudes and ways of living, highlighting differences that exist for other immigrant groups but which because other immigrant groups are the same colour as the indigenous population, go unnoticed. Undoubtedly colour prejudice exists in most areas, and the problems of integrating a sizeable coloured population are going to be difficult. Already there are important problems in education, in particular areas, over course of instruction, language, and differing beliefs and customs. In the labour and housing markets there are difficulties too.

But the difficulties exist; Britain is involved in the situation and progress towards a multi-racial society must proceed.

One more argument needs to be dealt with. This is the demand of immigrants for social services. It is often stated that the immigrants are a drag on the social services and that the Government might better spend the money on overseas aid to develop standards of living in the immigrants home countries. In fact, these arguments are fallacious largely because the majority of the immigrants come into the age ranges which do not demand many services from the different social services. Immigrants cost more per head of population in the number of births in hospital, education and child care, and tuberculosis, but they cost considerably less for hospitals, institutions and old people's homes, and mental care. The table below illustrates this point.

Internal Migration

The present distribution of the population of Britain is highly urbanized, with seven large conurbations claiming one third of the population. The following table and Figure 17 show the present population density and distribution.

The figures of the 1971 Census demonstrated that the distribution

72

of population was 76 per cent urban and 24 per cent rural, a 6 per cent movement to the countryside since the Census of 1961. The urban population is concentrated in seven conurbations, which between them have a population of 18·6 millions, one third of the total population.

In the fifteen years since the Census of 1961, the greatest rates of increase of population have occurred in the Outer South East, the Outer Metropolitan Area and East Anglia. Greater London has lost one million inhabitants during this period, as is shown in Figure 16.

It is interesting to trace the development of our present population

Cost per head of health and welfare services for home population and the immigrant population, 1961

| | Age Ranges | | | |
	Under 15	15–64	Over 65	Total
Age distribution of total population (46·1m) per cent	23·1	65·0	11·9	100·0
Age distribution of immigrant population (540,000) per cent	28·9	67·6	3·5	100·0
		(£ at 1961 prices)		
Social service cost per head of total population	20·2	14·0	39·3	18·5
Adjustments for the immigrant population:				
(a) Maternity care	+5·8			
(b) Tuberculosis and venereal diseases		+1·3		
(c) Different proportion of aged in institutions			−7·9	
(d) Mentally subnormal	−0·2	−0·8		
All adjustments	+5·6	+0·5	−7·9	
Social service cost per head of immigrant population	25·8	14·5	31·4	18·4
Comparison of social service cost of immigrant (compared with total population)	+5·6	+0·5	−7·9	−0·1

(Mrs. K. Jones, 'Immigrants and the Social Services', *National Institute Economic Review*, August 1967.)

Notes:
1. Total population is that for England and Wales.
2. Immigrant population is that from the New Commonwealth (the Caribbean, India and Pakistan, Africa, Cyprus and Malta).

distribution, to identify trends and the causes of the internal migration that has produced our present distribution.

Before the beginning of the process of industrialization, the population of England and Wales was very dispersed. There were only three large towns, London, Norwich and Bristol and the distribution of population reflected the important occupational distribution. Then England's economy was based on agricultural and the woollen industry. Three main areas primarily occupied themselves with the woollen trade – East Anglia, the Cotswolds and the West Riding – the first two being, at that stage, by far the most important. The 'capital' cities of these areas were Norwich and Bristol, which after the national capital, London, were the most important cities in the country.

By 1801 the distribution of population had undergone a profound change. No longer were the old woollen towns the most important cities in the country; in their stead had grown the new towns of the Midlands and the North. London still remained pre-eminent among cities, but the growth of an urban population surrounding its industry was reflected by the movement of population into the Midlands and the North.

A century later, in 1901, the southern drift had become a fact. The dark centre had spread southwards, as more and more people came to live in the largest city in the world, the centre of the greatest economic power and political power in the world. These changes can be compared by Figure 18.

At first glance the distribution of the population during this century has not changed very much. A distribution map drawn from the 1961 Census still shows the coffin-shaped zone of heavily urbanized population still stretching from Sussex to Lancashire and Yorkshire. All the counties within this zone contain an average of 450 people to the square mile. They account for only 31 per cent of the land area but for 72 per cent of the population, and over 73 per cent of the income.[1]

There have been important differences in detail within this general pattern. The main trend during this century has been the continued drift to the south. This, together with great differences in the rates of growth of population between the northern counties and the southern counties has produced a population imbalance, which is causing deep social and economic problems.

---

[1] 'Strategy for Planning', *New Society*, July 1966.

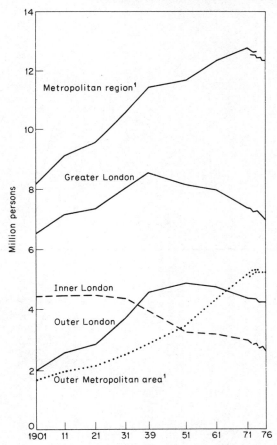

Fig. 16. *Population in the London Metropolitan Region, 1901–1976*

By the last years of the nineteenth century the drift to the northern towns, based on the growth industries of Britain's first period of industrialization, was being countered by the diminishing importance of coal as a source of power, the spread of electric power – and, as a consequence, the establishment of newer industries in locations better suited to their produce and market potential. These new industries, primarily in light engineering, consumer durable and service indus-

75

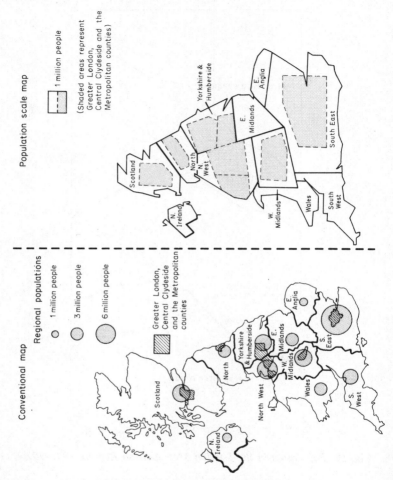

Fig. 17. *Population maps, United Kingdom, 1975*

tries preferred a location in the southern counties, in particular those of Essex, Kent, Hertfordshire, Sussex, Hampshire, Middlesex, Surrey, Bedfordshire and Buckinghamshire, to those of the north, whose industry scarred the dark and windswept moorlands. A more favour-

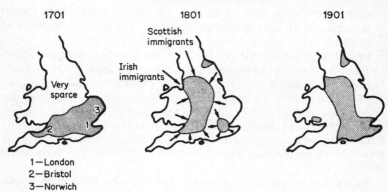

Fig. 18

able climate, more modern environment, market proximity to the growing population areas both at home and in Europe, and a well-defined and easy transport system centred on London, were all reasons why such industries preferred the south and the south east, to the more traditional industrial locations of the north.

No doubt social characteristics, nearness to a capital city with all its importance, better housing, better social amenities played a part too, but only as a peripheral reason to the central one of job opportunity, new opportunities and a willingness of men and women to participate in the growth areas of the economy from which the new opportunities will spring. These are the really important economic factors which determine an individual's mobility of labour from one geographical location to another. Individuals usually follow industry rather than the other way about; if industry locates in certain areas, its establishment will affect profoundly the industrial movement of population.

This drift to the south has created the South East Region, populated by seventeen millions, one third of the nation's population. As the South East Economic Planning Committee's plan 'A Strategy for the South East' published in 1967 states:

With the nation's capital in its centre, its people more than elsewhere think in national rather than regional terms. London dominates the region . . . as our capital (and) as a unique international

77

centre for commerce and finance, as well as world wide tourist attraction and as a centre for the arts, education, religion and science.

Into this region moved people from the northern counties, from Ireland, Scotland and abroad, to swell its population by 1½ millions between 1951–64. Since then the rate of growth has diminished slightly and in 1966 for the first time more people moved out of the region than moved into it. This was the result of a dwindling inflow from Ireland and Scotland, but even if we take the movements from other English regions alone we find the beginnings of a counter trend. More people have actually left the South East than have come into it.

As a result of the 'drift to the south' a growing imbalance of distribution of population between the north and the south has taken place. If we drew an imaginary line between Chester and Hull, Britain divides itself approximately into two equal halves by area. The 1961 Census showed that the northern counties held nineteen million people and the southern counties thirty-two millions. This in itself is a major imbalance, but the rates of growth suggest the problem is likely to grow worse in the future. Figure 19 illustrates this point.

Only the conurbation of Tyneside, South Lancashire, and the West and East Riding increased their population. Other than this, all population growth of any size took place in southern counties, principally in and around the South East and the South Midlands. This pattern of growth fits in with the fact that there is now a counter-trend away from the London area out into the surrounding counties; Berkshire is the county with the highest rate of post-war population growth in all Britain.

Two other major population features characterize recent internal changes in the internal distribution of population. They are the continued growth of the urban sprawl contained in the process of suburbanization, and the growth of conurbations, which have centred on an old established city and gradually extended themselves until they have taken over towns and villages around their perimeter.

There are now seven major conurbations in Britain whose populations are outlined in the table on page 68. Their growth has been continuous since the beginnings of industrial society, for they are the centres of the old nineteenth century distribution of population. London has always been the first city in the country, but neither of the other two medieval cities, Bristol and Norwich, is today a major conurbation, although Bristol might so develop by the end of the century. The South East Lancashire conurbation centres on Manchester, a city with a proud trading tradition and a fine Victorian city centre. The West Midlands is centred on Birmingham, after London the largest city in England. Central Clydeside's conurbation has Glasgow at its centre, a city with an important history of shipbuilding and heavy engineering. Merseyside is based on Liverpool, a few centuries ago a city of trade and slavery, today a city of trade and heavy engineering. Tyneside has long been famous for its central role in Britain's industrial history; the phrase 'taking coals to Newcastle' was no idle talk at a time when Newcastle exported the greatest part of our coal, the most important export of Britain right up until the

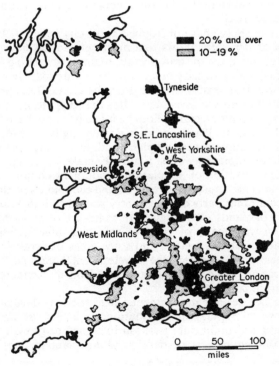

Fig. 19. *Population Increase 1951–61*

79

First World War. Today it is still the old heavy industries that dominate Tyneside, although in recent years some dispersal and change has taken place. West Yorkshire's 'capital' is Leeds with its townhall a true monument to Victorian pride and achievement. During this century all these major cities have gradually extended outwards until their rings extend up to forty miles into the country-side in the case of London and twenty miles in the case of Manchester or Birmingham.[1] As well as the towns expanding, the population within the towns has moved too. The heart of the cities are becoming dead places as their inhabitants move outwards, first into the inner suburbs, and then further out again, to the outer suburbs and the suburban ring. This movement too is an imbalance which causes problems. If the process continues, British city centres will become as drab and lifeless as their American counterparts, and as strictly structured between industrial areas, commercial areas, amenity areas and housing areas.

The urban sprawl has not stopped at the city fringe. J. J. Moran in his study of Berkshire shows that most new houses have been built along the corridors of transportation lines 'stretching in discon-tinuous fashion up to sixty miles into the countryside. In comparison with the dominance of these corridors, the Green Belt appears insig-nificant to the point of invisibility'. It is the recognition of this sprawl along major communication lines that has prompted the South East Regional Economic Planning Council to try to plan ahead, move with the trend into the counties and plan South East along lines dominated by communications networks. Figure 20 makes this clear.

This concentration of population in southern counties and in the conurbations has caused severe social and economic imbalance which has affected other parts of the country severely. Both Wales and the Western Highlands of Scotland are examples of areas of declining population with many of the problems that afflict classic cases of depopulation such as Ireland and some areas of rural France. To a lesser extent the problems of the Development Areas and the so-called 'grey' areas are afflicted by the same problems of declining industries and emigrant populations.

In this last respect governments have tried to develop a logical policy toward population distribution. It is just as important as establishing an equilibrium position in regard to growth of popula-tion. If this country is to develop along planned lines of logical

---

[1] J. J. Moran, *New Society*, July 18, 1966.

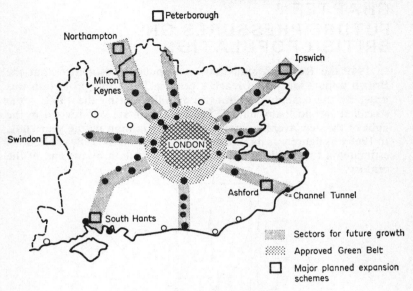

Fig. 20. *A Strategy for the South East*
(HMSO. 1967)

development, a population policy designed to effect both growth equilibrium and distribution equilibrium is needed urgently.

81

CHAPTER 6
FUTURE PRESSURES ON
BRITISH POPULATION

In 1949 the Royal Commission on Population estimated that the British population would reach a peak in 1977; this projection was upset by the changing fashion for families during the 1960s – the so-called second 'baby bulge'. The 1964 estimate was revised in the light of the new average family size to 75½ million by the year 2001. In 1968 this figure was modified to 68 million and the 1969 projections estimated a further drop in the total of £½ million by the end of the century.

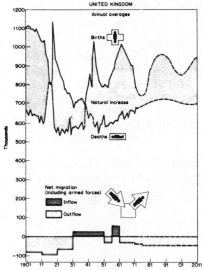

Fig. 21. *Population changes*

The nation's demographers have become so used to being wrong that now they present projections in three fertility variants – a principal projection, high short term fertility and low short term fertility. Present projections of the population of Great Britain are 55·9 million, 56·6 million and 54·9 million, growth of 1·4 million, 2·1 million or 0·4 million on the 1976 population of 54·5 million. These figures are much lower than the 20 per cent, 11 million growth, predicted in 1969. The projections are tabulated below.

82

Population changes and projections
United Kingdom

Millions and thousands

	Census enumerated				Mid-year estimates				Projections¹		
	1901 -11	1911 -31	1931 -51	1951 -61	1961 -66	1966 -71	1971 -76	1976 -77²	1975 -81	1981 -91	1991 -2001
Home population (millions) at start of period	38·2	42·1	46·0	50·3	52·8	54·5	55·6	55·9	56·0	55·7	56·7
Average annual change (thousands):											
Live births	1,091	899	785	839	988	937	766	..	657	856	839
Deaths	624	622³	598³	593	633	644	670	..	686	714	717
Net natural change	467	277	188	246	355	293	96	..	-29	142	122
Net civilian migration	} -82	-79	+22	-7	-8	-56	-45	..	} -32	-40	
Other net changes				+13	-8⁴	-16⁴	13⁴	..			
Overall annual change	385	198	213	252	339	222	64	..	-61	102	82

¹ Projections based on the mid-1976 estimate of *total* population.
² Provisional.
³ Including deaths of non-civilians and merchant seamen who died outside the country.
⁴ The England and Wales component includes changes in armed forces and in visitor balance and balancing adjustments to reconcile population increase with estimates of natural increase and net civilian migration.

Sources: Census of Population Reports: Population Projections 1976-2016, *Office of Population Censuses and Surveys*

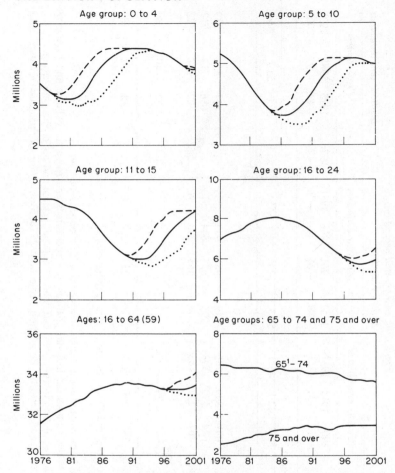

Fig. 22. *1977 based population projections on the short-term fertility assumptions: by age groups*

Population projections are notably open to error. It is important therefore to analyse in some detail the factors affecting these projections and to understand why the projections have been modified during the last six years. The first approach is to examine past trends and see if these can be projected forward, or whether they are going to change in the future.

Death rates are assumed to follow past trends quite closely. Very recently, they have been practically stationary, but over the next thirty years it is assumed that they will continue the steady downward path experienced during the last half century. This projection assumes an increase in knowledge relating to general health and medical practice. Some caution should be exercised here, for it is possible that with the stress occasioned by the pressures of modern life, the death rate might even rise – the life expectancy in the USA actually fell in 1969. On the other hand major new advances in medical knowledge could lower the death rate of the middle age groups which fall proportionately more slowly than the young and infant death rates, thus producing a significant effect on the overall pattern.

Migration produces a net outflow of about 20,000 a year. As we have seen, after the very large net inflows from the Commonwealth during the fifties, recent years have seen a marginal reversal of the trends. This has occurred because of the introduction of immigration controls and a new impetus to emigrate to the older Commonwealth countries. It is unlikely that immigration control will be relaxed during the next thirty years, so that present trends are expected to be maintained. Although at present immigrants appear to have a greater fertility than the emigrants they replace, this greater fertility is offset by the smaller numbers involved.

Birth rates are always the most difficult population statistic to predict, a fact which is amply illustrated by the experience of the Aberfan community in South Wales, after the experience of a random event, the Aberfan Colliery disaster, which in 1966 killed 116 children and 28 adults. The table below shows that about 130 more children were born than would have been expected on the basis of area average.

Birth rates must be closely studied. Factors which influence birth rate are shown in Figure 24, and may be enumerated under five heads – the base consisting of the number of women of child-bearing age, the attitudes to marriage, the average family size, divorce and illegitimacy.

The two base factors determining birth rates are the number of women of the child-bearing age groups 15–45 years, and the number of children women have during the child-bearing period. The number of women of the child-bearing age groups can be determined over a thirty-year period – because all the women who will form that

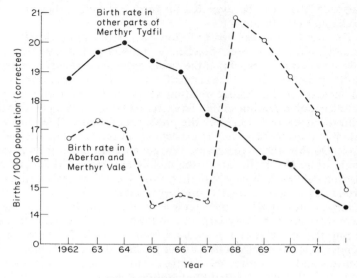

Fig. 23. Source: *Guardian*

group until late in the century, are alive today. For instance, the females born between 1960–69 will be the important child-bearing group in the 1980s. Progress from the base factor to the ultimate number of children per woman during the child-bearing years is more difficult to predict and is subject to a variety of conflicting pressures.

The vast majority of children are born within marriage, so that the married state can be taken as the norm for the bearing of children. The importance of marriage to population increase is measured by popularity of marriage – the number of people who marry, and the age at which people become married. If the age of marriage is higher, the number of fertile years, when a woman is 'at risk' will be less; if the age of marriage is lowered, the number of fertile years increases, and it is likely, other things being equal, that a larger number of children will result from the union.

The factors bearing on the 'fashion for families' are multitudinous and often conflicting and they have already been discussed in the historical context of British population growth. The average real income of families, the possibility of equal pay for women, the

86

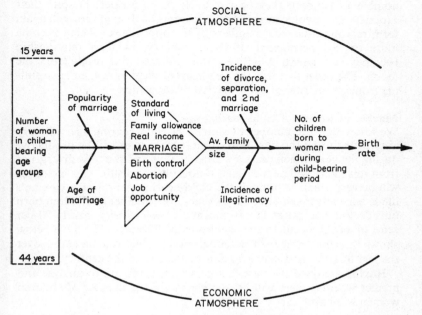

Fig. 24. *Factors Affecting the Birth Rate*

importance of the wife working in addition to the husband, thereby bringing in quite a large second income, the real and supposed standard of living of the family and the effect that a child will have on that standard of living, must all be balanced against social factors, such as the provision of welfare assistance by social services – provision of nursery schools, free milk, national health service, family allowances, the availability of contraception and abortion.

These factors will affect the average family size: it is this figure that is basic to the determination of the birth rate and population projections. However, two other factors must be brought to bear on the situation before we can estimate the figure of the number of children women will have during their child-bearing period.

The incidence of divorce, separation and re-marriage will have some bearing on the figures. If women are going to be involved with two or more families during their child-bearing years, then the

87

number of children they bear is likely to be greater. Despite their experience of divorce or separation it seems likely that they will again form relationships with members of the opposite sex which become more or less permanent. If they re-marry, or their relationship becomes permanent, it is likely that children will result from the union. The other factor is the incidence of illegitimacy, either resulting from pre-marital or extra-marital relationships.

Number of women of child-bearing age

We know that the number of women of child-bearing age will vary very little during the next thirty years; those who will be productive during the next fifteen years are already alive and the only divergence from this figure will be the result of infertility or death. This incidence will be very small. Although the child-bearing period of a woman's life is normally taken to be 15–44 years – the number of children born outside this age range is insignificant – the majority, nearly 70 per cent, of births occur to the age group 20–29 years. The table below shows that the number of potential mothers will remain stable over the last quarter, and may even fall by the end of the century.

Having analysed the base factor, we must now try to analyse and predict whether there will be any change in the number of children women will have.

Attitudes to marriage

For forty years before 1911, marriage rates among women were declining. Between 1911 and the end of the 1960s a remarkable turnabout took place; there has been an increase of nearly one-third in the proportion of women aged 20–40, who were married between 1911–54. Richard Titmuss in *Essays on the Welfare State* comments, 'Never before, in the history of English vital statistics, has there been such a high proportion of married women in the female population under the age of forty and even more so under the age of thirty.'

Figs. 25 and 26 show this marked lowering of the average age of marriage and the increasing popularity of marriage amongst women of all age groups. In the past, these factors have always been taken as a potential pressure to increase the number of children born during the marriage, because of the longer number of years the wife will be 'at risk'. Today, with improved methods of family planning, this may not be such an important factor, but it must still be borne in mind that its effect will be towards a higher birth rate.

Fig. 24 shows that whatever attacks are made on the institution

Sex and age structure of the population[1]
United Kingdom

Various units

	Census enumerated				Mid-year estimates					Projections[2,3]		
	1901	1911	1921	1931	1941	1951	1961	1971	1976[4]	1981	1991	2001
By sex and age group (millions):												
Males:												
Under 15	6·2	6·5	6·2	5·6	5·1	5·8	6·3	6·9	6·6	5·8	5·9	6·4
15–29	5·2	5·4	5·3	5·8	5·8	5·3	5·3	6·0	6·3	6·6	6·6	5·5
30–44	3·6	4·3	4·3	4·5	5·5	5·5	5·3	4·9	5·0	5·5	6·0	6·6
45–64[5]	2·7	3·2	4·1	4·6	5·0	5·6	6·4	6·5	6·3	6·1	6·0	6·6
65–74	0·6	0·7	0·9	1·1	1·4	1·6	1·6	2·0	2·2	2·2	2·2	2·0
75 and over	0·2	0·2	0·3	0·3	0·5	0·7	0·7	0·8	0·9	1·0	1·2	1·2
All ages	18·5	20·4	21·0	22·1	23·3	24·4	25·7	27·1	27·3	27·2	27·8	28·4
Females:												
Under 15	6·2	6·5	6·1	5·5	5·0	5·6	6·0	6·5	6·2	5·5	5·6	6·1
15–29	5·6	5·8	5·9	6·0	5·8	5·2	5·1	5·8	6·0	6·2	6·2	5·2
30–44	3·9	4·6	5·0	5·2	5·8	5·7	5·3	4·8	4·9	5·4	5·8	6·3
45–59[5]	2·4	2·9	3·6	4·2	4·6	5·1	5·5	5·2	5·0	4·8	4·6	5·3
60–74	1·3	1·5	1·9	2·4	3·0	3·5	3·9	4·5	4·5	4·5	4·2	3·8
75 and over	0·3	0·4	0·5	0·5	0·8	1·1	1·5	1·8	2·0	2·2	2·4	2·4
All ages	19·7	21·7	23·0	24·0	24·9	26·1	27·3	28·6	28·7	28·6	28·9	29·2

Sex ratio
(males per 1,000 females):

All ages	937	937	915	920	933	934	941	947	950	953	962	971
Under 45 years	955	957	928	949	990	1,008	1,027	1,038	1,043	1,045	1,049	1,052
45 years and over	866	869	877	852	819	808	811	810	812	815	827	849

By country (millions):

England and Wales	32·5	36·1	37·9	40·0	41·7	44·0	46·3	48·9	49·2	49·0	49·8	50·6
Scotland	4·5	4·8	4·9	4·8	5·2	5·2	5·2	5·2	5·2	5·2	5·3	5·4
Northern Ireland	1·2	1·2	1·3[6]	1·2[6]	1·3	1·4	1·4	1·5	1·5	1·5	1·6	1·6
United Kingdom	38·2	42·1	44·0	46·0	48·2	50·6	53·0	55·7	56·0	55·7	56·7	57·5

Note: See also Table 1.9 (International comparisons).

[1] Figures relate to the census enumerated population until 1931, thereafter they relate to the *total* population. See also notes in Appendix.

[2] Figures in italics are based partly on the assumptions made about future fertility rates.

[3] 1976 based.

[4] Provisional.

[5] Retirement ages 65 and over for men, 60 and over for women.

[6] Mid-year estimates; a census was not taken in Northern Ireland in 1921 and 1931.

Sources: Census of Population Reports: Population Projections, 1976–2016, *Office of Population Censuses and Surveys*.

of marriage, the institution itself is increasing in popularity.

The trend remarked upon by Professor Titmuss extended into the 1960s. Michael Schofield, in his analysis of teenage society, *The Sexual Behaviour of Young People*, further emphasizes that marriage is very definitely not outmoded. Out of his survey only 6 per cent of the younger boys (15–17 years) and 3 per cent of the older boys (17–19 years), said they did not want to marry, and hardly any of the girls (1 per cent in each age group) stated the same. He stressed that there was a big difference between the sexes as to the ideal time to marry (35 per cent of the younger and 43 per cent of the older boys said

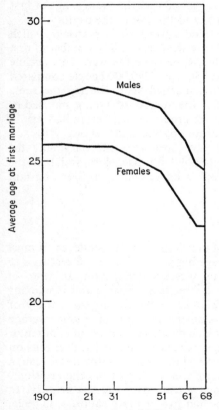

Fig. 25. *Average Age of Marriage* (*Social Trends*, 1971)

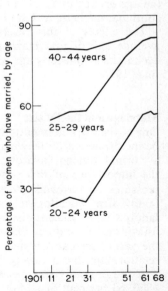

Fig. 26 *Percentage of Women Married* (*Social Trends*, 1971)

91

they did not want to marry before the age of twenty-five, whilst only 9 per cent of the girls in both age groups said the same). Over a third (38 per cent) of the younger girls wanted to marry before the age of twenty-one, and one in four of all boys and girls agreed with the statement that 'girls believe today that, if they are not married before they are twenty-one, they are on the shelf.'

At the end of the 1960s it was expected that the increase in the number of marriages would continue, as would the lowering of the average age of a first marriage. Not only was the trend established, but recent social legislation, such as the Age of Majority Bill (1970) and the Equal Pay and Equal Opportunities Acts, together with the lowering of the age of puberty, suggested that the average age of first marriage would continue to decline to the end of the century.

The 1970s, however, saw the trend towards early marriage, which had continued since before the last war, reversed. The number of first marriages fell in 1973 for the first time since the war. This decline continued to the present year (1975), when 296,000 people compared with 357,000 in 1971 entered the married state. During the same period small falls were recorded in the number of women married in the age groups up to about 25, age groups which before had seen a continual increase, a trend illustrated by the chart below.

The effects of this reversal have been to raise marginally the average age of first marriage to 24·9 for bachelors and halt the decline in a spinster's age at 22·7, a figure which has been constant since 1971.

Marriage and family size

One of the avowed intentions of marriage is to have children. It must be the prime reason why marriage has survived over the centuries as a normal human institution in Western civilization. In spite of the importance of this raison d'etre, there exist many conflicting pressures on husband and wife which make for a great variety of family size. Sociologists and statisticians, talking about average family size, produce statistics, which divide into halves of children or four-fifths of children. These figures conceal important decisions on the part of men and women involved in the most intimate of human relationships and a variety of numbers resulting from the decisions.

Average family size has varied greatly over the last century. In 1860, 63 per cent of all families had five or more children; in 1925, 67 per cent of families had two or less children. Since the inter-war period the average family size has been on the increase. The table below shows the trend during the last forty years.

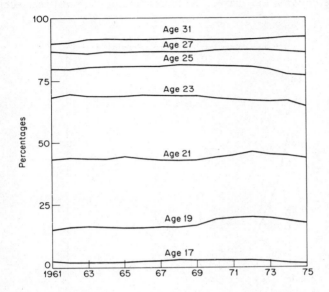

Fig. 27. *Percentages of women married by different ages. 1961–1975*

At the beginning of the 1970s the average completed family size was 2·4 children per household. More detailed studies, involving projections of family size for brides marrying at the age of 20 or younger suggested that their completed family size would be 2·88, a figure which contrasted with 3·4 children forecast at the height of the birth rate boom in 1964.

The trend towards a smaller family size has continued during the 1970s. The tables below show that couples are delaying the birth of a first child longer and the number of households having a third or later children have also fallen. As a consequence, the average family size has fallen to 2·07 children per household, a figure comparable with pre-war levels of family building.

Elizabeth Still conducting enquiries into family size reveals in an article in *New Society* (June 8, 1967) that 'it is no longer true that the lower down the social scale and the less educated people are, the more children they have. The inverse relationship between social

Fig. 28. *The English family*
(*The Economist*)

This chart shows the average number of children born, or expected to be born, to women in England and Wales married in each year since 1920. This is the completed family size – not the average number of children in English homes at any one time. Obviously guesswork comes into recent figures since all the women married in these years will not have finished having children. Projections are based on recent fertility rates.

class and family size seems to be disappearing fast.' In the 1920s and 1930s, the typical professional or upper middle class family had one or two children. During the 1960s, four became an increasingly fashionable number. This fact is borne out in the table on page 97.

Legitimate live births to women married once only: by number of previous liveborn children
England and Wales

Thousands and percentages

Number of previous liveborn children:	Live births (thousands)					Percentage change from preceding year				
	1972	1973	1974	1975	1976	1972	1973	1974	1975	1976
0	262·2	249·3	237·6	221·5	211·2	− 6·5	− 4·9	− 4·7	− 6·8	− 4·7
1	223·9	215·8	208·3	198·4	195·1	− 4·8	− 3·6	− 3·5	− 4·8	− 1·6
2	93·6	80·5	71·8	67·1	64·4	−12·4	−14·0	−10·8	− 6·5	− 4·0
3	36·3	29·5	24·7	22·1	20·3	−15·3	−18·8	−16·3	−10·5	− 8·4
4	14·2	10·9	9·0	7·8	7·0	−18·6	−22·9	−17·8	−13·5	− 9·7
5 and over	12·2	9·4	7·5	6·6	5·9	−21·1	−22·8	−19·7	−13·0	−10·8
Total	642·3	595·4	558·9	523·4	503·8	− 8·0	− 7·3	− 6·1	− 6·3	− 3·7

Source: Office of Population Censuses and Surveys

Average family size at specified durations of marriage
Great Britain

	Year of marriage							Average		
	1935 –39	1940 –44	1945 –49	1950 –54	1955 –59	1960 –64	1965 –69	1971	1972	1973
Average number of live births[1] at marriage duration:										
2 years	0·55	0·50	0·65	0·60	0·63	0·69	0·64	0·52	0·48	0·46
5 years	1·05	1·10	1·26	1·24	1·37	1·48	1·37			
10 years	1·67	1·73	1·83	1·92	2·07	2·10				
15 years	1·96	1·98	2·11	2·20	2·30					
Completed family size	2·07	2·09	2·22	2·30	2·38[2]					

[1] To women married once only before the age of 45.
[2] Estimate.

Source: Office of Population Censuses and Surveys

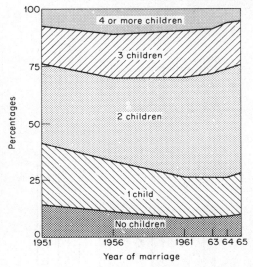

Fig. 29. *Family size distributions after 10 years of marriage*

Mean family size after 15–19 and 25–29 years of marriage in 1961 (all ages at marriage under 45) by ages at which husband and wife completed education

years of marriage	age of wife on completing education	age of husband on completing education				year of marriage
		under 15	15–16	17–19	20+	
15–19	under 15	2·09	1·91	1·88	1·92	1943–47
25–29		2·10	1·83	1·71	1·79	1933–37
15–19	15–16	1·90	1·88	1·87	2·01	1943–47
25–29		1·82	1·69	1·65	1·65	1933–47
15–19	17–19	1·85	1·85	1·91	2·17	1943–47
25–29		1·73	1·67	1·73	1·87	1933–47
15–19	20+	1·68	1·55	1·93	2·15	1943–47
25–29		1·51	1·59	1·78	1·88	1933–47

Source: New Society, 8 June 1967

Since the sixties, the trend for larger families in professional classes has declined, although the overall decline is offset by a rising number of people within this class category. The biggest change has been a fall in the number of births of third or later children born to manual workers, although this pattern is similar in all classes.

The reversal of family building patterns established over the period 1941–64 should not be seen only in the context of the United King-

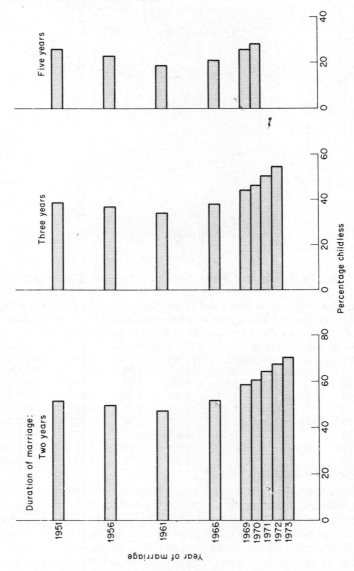

Fig. 30 *Women childless by duration of marriage*

dom; our experience is part of a change in family decision-making experienced by most developed countries in Europe and across the North American continent, evidence of which is provided by comparative birth rates in these countries illustrated below.

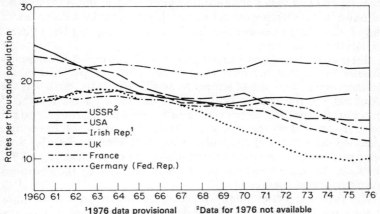

¹1976 data provisional   ²Data for 1976 not available

Fig. 31. *Birth rates: international comparison*

Source: *UN Demographic Yearbook 1974.* Reproduced by permission.

The complex mix of reasons behind the decision of families to have fewer children may be considered under four headings – the process of continual modernization, changing economic factors, changing social attitudes and the improvement in family planning services.

The notion that this decline in the number of children couples choose to have is entirely due to increasing use and knowledge of methods of family planning is too easy an answer. Nevertheless, the increasing awareness and understanding of such methods is important. It has allowed husbands and wives greater power of decision-making over the size of their family; and, it has allowed couples the freedom to react to changing economic factors and social attitudes, by being able to make responsible decisions.

The acceptance of contraceptives is an important development in population projection. If contraceptives became technically 100 per cent efficient, as well as being humanly 100 per cent efficient, then average families would have more than just a statistical meaning. Such is not yet the case. It is still true that families of higher occupation status understand and use contraceptives better than families of manual workers, who tend to be less well educated, and thus do not or will not use contraceptives, but the trend shows a marked increase in the use of contraceptives by men and women of all classes.

Attitudes to and efficient use of contraceptives have an important bearing on the number of unwanted children born. But if the number of unwanted children were cut to zero it would make a difference of only 0·13 children per average family, which would not be sufficient to halt the increasing population.

Surveys by Dr. Anne Cartwright of the Institute of Community Studies found that for their most recent birth, 15 per cent of the mothers were 'sorry it had happened at all'. Where the birth was the third baby in the family, 19 per cent were sorry, for the fourth, 25 per cent; for the fifth, 39 per cent; and for later births, roughly 50 per cent. It seems likely that the legalization of abortion will have some effect on the number of unwanted children. In 1969, 54,000 abortions were performed under the Act, and thousands more illegally, in 1972 the figure for legal abortions was 167,000. In 1975, 63,100 abortions were performed legally.

The fact that better family planning services exist allows more couples the luxury of responsible decision-making, and it avoids a number of unwanted children. But, as Dr. Cartwright has pointed out, the significance of cutting the number of unwanted children is very marginal.

The process which demographers call 'modernization' is a long term trend which affects all developed countries when their economic and social systems reach the mature period of their life-cycle. It is a process which aggregates millions of individual – and seemingly unconnected – decisions into a social trend of some consequence. As an economy develops, improvements in medicine control death and the infant mortality rates. For a time, population increases but, as members of the society become more aware of technical and social changes bearing on the decision to have children, they adjust, each for its own reason, but as part of a general trend. Thus, the fact that children are no longer needed to till land because the economic system has become industrial rather than agricultural is added to the need for longer educational careers, greater economic opportunities both for men and women, which in turn leads to delaying the age of marriage and finally to the decision to have smaller families.

Most developed countries have experienced inflation throughout the late sixties and seventies. Inflation is a major deterrent. The cost of having children has risen dramatically: as incomes have not in-

*Current use of contraceptives: by year of marriage and social class, 1975
England and Wales*

Percentages

	Condom	Pill	With-drawal	Safe period	Cap	Inter-uterine device	Other	Absti-nence	None	Total sample[1] size (= 100%) (numbers)
Year of first marriage										
1956–60	28	29	11	1	3	8	4	1	17	309
1961–65	29	34	8	2	3	10	5	2	11	400
1966–70	26	44	5	1	4	11	4	1	9	485
1971–75	17	60	6	1	2	5	2	1	8	404
Social class										
Non-manual	28	42	4	1	5	9	4	2	9	672
Manual:										
III	24	43	8	1	2	9	4	1	12	707
IV and V	24	39	13	1	1	7	4	1	14	276
Total	24	42	9	1	1	8	4	1	13	983

[1] Sample = ever married fecund women under 41 years who were neither pregnant nor trying to conceive.
Source: Family Planning Services Survey, *Department of Health and Social Security*

creased by the same amount while unemployment rates have risen, the *real* cost of a child is now examined much more critically than before. In recent years, the real cost – the opportunity cost – has become too great for an increasing number of couples. Interwoven through this greater awareness of economic realities are the changing social attitudes produced by a period of history which has seen sometimes conflicting and often bewildering changes.

The prevailing experience, for most people, has been an increase in economic and social freedoms and opportunity. The freedom to travel world-wide, to participate in intellectual and physical leisure pursuits, previously only the province of the wealthy, to buy increasingly expensive consumer durables and to increase the quality of living within the household budget, combined with the increasing employment opportunities for both men and women, have made many more families count the cost of a child more accurately. As an American couple living in Cambridge, Massachusetts who both work, and who enjoy their work as well as expensive leisure pursuits such as skiing, put it: 'It takes a lot of money to stretch the goodies around.' They have one small child and are not sure they will have any more! (Quote from *Time Magazine*, 16 September 1974.)

Social attitudes have changed remarkably, some would say in a way amounting to a small revolution. The complex of changes and emotions under the collective heading 'Women's Lib' has made its contribution. This movement has encouraged women to challenge their traditional roles as mother and housewife, has brought into greater relief the satisfaction to be gained from a successful career and has made acceptable the idea that a woman can still be a woman even if she does not want children. At the same time, increasing concern of over-population and environmental destruction have made respectable an attitude which proclaims that small families are best. The *Time Magazine* article referred to above also recounts an interview with a mother in Madison, New Jersey, who has eight children who stated that she frequently encounters hostility on the grounds that her brood 'consumed too much oxygen and too much space'. Similar attitudes may help to explain the decrease in British family size.

Divorce and illegitimacy

Both the rate of divorce and of illegitimacy are significant trends.

The number of divorce decrees issued in England and Wales has increased enormously. In 1931, there were 3,668; in 1951, 28,265; by

102

1971 this had jumped to 74,400 and this, by 1976, had increased to 120,500. The rate per thousand of married population had increased from 2·6 per cent in 1951 to 9·6 per cent in 1976.

However, these figures must be put into perspective. A large number of divorces occur after the woman has passed the child-bearing age and cannot therefore affect population size. Similarly, the illegitimacy rate must not be overstressed, even though illegitimate births as a proportion of total births have increased from 8·4 per cent in 1971 to 9·2 per cent in 1976. More significant perhaps may be the rates of increase, which are declining over the period from 1971–76 compared with 1961–71 (9·5 per cent compared with 44 per cent).

Pressure of population in Britain

Changes in the patterns of population are cumulative. As a snake devours a meal, the bulge passes down its body as digestion takes place; changes in population at any one time proceed to produce different problems and pressures at different times. Thus, the pressure of population on educational services is felt first in the primary sector, but twenty years later, the pressure is felt in the higher education field. As with education so with other social services.

Although changes in population do cause changes in demand for resources, it should be noted that, as important, is the size of population multiplied by the income per head. Thus, a decline in population does not of itself cause a drop in demand for resources, unless the income per head, the ability to demand resources, drops too. Thus, as Britain's total population growth decreases, the drop in demand for resources will change only marginally, unless there is a complementary switch in life style to what John Vaizey has described as a high technology 'simple' life that economizes in natural resources, including space. (John Vaizey 'The effects of population size', *New Society*, June 7, 1973.) This fact has also been noted by the Government 'Think Tank' which acknowledges that the demand for services operates rather like the Ratchet Effect on Wages – they tend to increase but not to decrease.

At the beginning of the seventies the fear was overpopulation. Although it was difficult to see the classic primary 'Malthusian' effects gripping a well-developed country like Britain, the secondary effects and the effects on supply of natural resources appeared likely to increase in significance. During the seventies important changes have taken place in the balance of the pressures, although the overall pressure on resources remains.

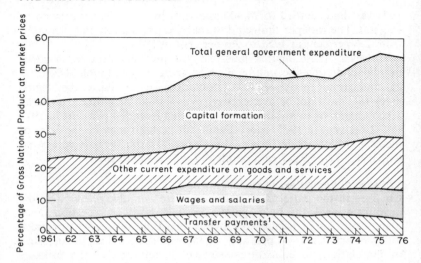

Fig. 32. *General government expenditure 1961–76: by economic category*

Britain is likely to experience an ageing population between now and the end of the century, but the dependent population is unlikely to increase as quickly as fewer babies are born and women become a more important section of the working population. At first sight this change may appear to reduce the burden on the social services but practice suggests the opposite. The Think Tank's 1977 publication *Population and the Social Services* suggests 'Rising numbers generate demands for proportionately more expenditure; static (or relatively declining) numbers do not yield proportional savings . . . in spite of the increased expenditure on social policy the needs are far from satisfied.'

Thus, although there will be changes in content – the demand for primary schools is now significantly lower than a decade ago, the demand for maternity beds similarly reduced, at the same time the demand for pensions is increasing, as is the pressure on places in higher education – the overall problem of financing the social services remains. With inflation likely to continue well into the eighties, the problems of budgeting, tax raising and forward planning, as well as the complex problem of switching resources from one use to another, will be critical.

Investment ratios 1955–64

Rank by growth rate	Investment ratio per cent of GNP	Investment ratio per cent of GNP excluding dwellings
Japan	28·8	21·5*
West Germany	23·7	18·4
Italy	21·6	15·6
Sweden	22·8	17·4
France	19·2	14·3
Denmark	18·7	15·4
Belgium	18·4	13·7
USA	17·1	12·2
UK	15·8	12·7

* *NEDO* estimate 1955–63.

(DEA Report, No. 21a)

Whether this figure can be increased between now and the end of the century is one of the major economic problems facing all governments.[1]

The dependent population is likely to increase too. The burden is already large, but will increase by the end of the century causing additional problems in economic and social planning and government control.

The rise in the population is likely to cause future balance of payments problems. An increase in population leads to a rise in aggregate money demand, and the level of imports is a direct function of the level of aggregate money demand. Even if the proportion of our food bill supplied by imported foodstuffs does not increase, we are going to be faced with an increase in imports. A rise in the import bill will increase the need to increase exports and this may only be able to be achieved by a large switch of investment and production into export industries such as occurred during the 1966–70 balance of payments crisis, which was accompanied by a stagnancy in the standard of living and domestic growth rates that worried everyone.

A major consequence will be on the level of public expenditure. Already public expenditure plays a major part in total aggregate

---

[1] See *National Income and Expenditure in Britain and OECD*, S. Hayes, H.E.B.

money demand. Problems of budgeting, tax raising and forward planning are already apparent. With a rise in population these will increase. The increase in the dependent population will increase demand for public services of all kinds.

Major areas of concern are the levels of education spending, public health expenditure and the social services and pensions extended to old people.

In education, the increase in the school population will inevitably be translated into a shortage of teachers, the continuance of over-size classes, continuing shortage of resources, shortage of nursery schools and further education colleges. One estimate made in 1964 by A. E. Holmans for the *London & Cambridge Economic Bulletin*, projected an increase of 45 per cent, assuming no decrease in the size of classes, or change in the school leaving age.

The impact of rising population on health services is measured by the rise in total expenditure, by the demand for hospital beds, maternity places and the proportion of doctors per head of population. Estimate of the number of hospital beds required sees an increase of 20,000 for every fifteen years assuming a rate of growth of population as at present. The demand for maternity places is even greater, an extra 135,000 every fifteen years. As medical education becomes more costly and more technical, the supply of doctors diminishes – and the ratio of doctors per head of population decreases. It is unlikely that we will reach the level of one African country, where there are five indigenous doctors for a population of three millions, but any de-crease in the proportion will inevitably put great strain upon resources.

An increasingly dependent population means an increasing public expenditure on pensions which are financed by the working popula-tion through National Insurance contributions. Such a system is very right and proper but an increase in the quantity and the quality of services to old people inevitably increases the strain on resources. A look at the table above on patterns of public expenditure through the 1960s shows the increased burden placed on public expenditure by social security benefits. This will increase proportionately through to the end of the century.

Land use
Britain at present produces 50 per cent of her food requirements and imports the rest from overseas. To support an increasing population,

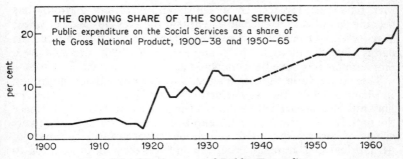

Fig. 33. *Patterns of Public Expenditure*
(DEA Report, No. 29)

rising to 66½ millions by the end of the century, she will have to intensify the methods by which she raises food from the soil, or be prepared to increase her import bill. At the same time land is needed for housing. Every year, at the present rate of increase, 44,000 acres of agricultural land are lost in urban development – in ten years an area the size of Worcestershire is swallowed by urban growth. P. A. Stone has calculated that an area of 350 acres per 10,000 of population is a reasonable figure to take as an estimate of land requirements. This means that by the end of the century another 385,000 acres will be taken in by urban growth – and this is additional to land required for housing.[1]

Large though this figure appears it still represents only 5 per cent of total agricultural land in the United Kingdom. Despite the fact that much of it is likely to be good agricultural land, there is still not a great cause for alarm, except in highly populated areas of the Midlands and the southern counties, where the Green Belt has been plundered for new housing development three times since 1967.

If agriculture is to succeed in reaching its targets without increasing the import bill and working on a diminishing land area, it must increase the productivity of the land it uses. Almost unnoticed by the urban population a revolution in agricultural techniques has been taking place throughout this century. Net output per acre has been rising by about 2·9 per cent per annum and this at a time when the number of men employed by the industry has continued to decline.

---

[1] P. A. Stone, 'Economics of Housing and Urban Development', *Journal of Royal Stats. Soc.*, (*Vol. 22*).

Men have been replaced by machines and fertilizers. Farming has become an industry to such an extent that the average yields of wheat have increased from 19·1 cwt to 28·2 cwts per acre in 1968–69, and the barley yield has increased from an average of 17·8 cwt to 27·4 cwts. Similar increases have been shown in all other products.

There seems little doubt that agriculture can take care of the growth in demand. But the side-effects of this increased productivity may not be as beneficial as the food produced. In order to increase the production, farming will have to be further intensified. The likely effects of this are that more and more hedgerows will be removed, perhaps causing drainage problems and soil erosion, in addition to reducing the diversity of living species which depend on the hedgerows for life. Yields from the land may begin to fall as the nutrients are removed from the soil. Disease amongst animals may increase as they are herded together in greater concentration. And this disease may not be so easily wiped out as bacterial strains become immune to drugs.

Housing

The fear expressed by L. Needleham in 'A Long Term View of Housing' (NIESR, November 1961) was that an extra 12·2 million houses would be required between 1961 and the end of the century. This projection assumed that population increase would continue and is therefore wrong by presently available statistics. But the problems of housing, if different, remain.

Whilst there is likely to be a surplus of houses being built in Britain over the next few years, the demand for housing will not decrease just because population decreases or becomes stable. The demand for houses is very much determined by income levels, by life styles and social attitudes. Demand may be changed by the number of people who prefer to live on their own – young as well as old – the number of persons who demand more than one house, the type of house which is in demand and by the changing distribution of population, particularly the continued movement away from city centres. Thus the problem of housing remains.

Resources

Britain is richer in resources than she was a decade ago. Not only have reserves of oil been found in abundance in the North Sea, but new finds of coal in Yorkshire (Selby) and the Vale of Belvoir (Leicestershire) mean that we could be self sufficient in energy

108

beyond the end of the century, a considerable improvement on the 1969 position. Nevertheless Britain remains weak in supplies of important raw materials vital to her industries. Desposits of iron ore are almost worked out and are of an inferior quality. China clay and building materials are also under severe pressure. Timber supplies are amongst the poorest in Europe, and necessitate an import of 90 per cent of total timber requirements.[1]

Demand for all these resources will increase as the demand on industry to increase production, and the primary demands of an increasing population, increase. Sand and gravel will be lifted from the earth at the rate of 120 million tons a year until the end of the century. Demand by the Government to increase land under forest will require another 40,000 acres a year to be diverted from agricultural purposes. The present demand for water is approximately 25 million gallons per day against a total rainfall of only 50 million gallons. It is expected that demand will increase to between 60–70 millions a day before the end of the century.[2]

Environment

The activities of the National Trust and the Conservation Society make it very clear that unless we work hard to preserve areas of natural beauty, the demands of an urban-industrialized society will sweep them away. These areas are limited. Even at our present level of population the demand is almost too great to bear. Think of the crowds with their litter that descend on the National Parks and other beauty spots each holiday season. Remember the traffic jams and the amount of land that is taken up by the demand of the motor vehicle! Think – and multiply the demand by the increase in the population!

Demand for all types of recreational and leisure facility will increase. This too will have to be taken from a fixed amount of land, give or take the marginal amount that can be brought back into use by reclamation schemes. If, as is assumed, the larger part of our projected increase in population lives in an urban community, there will be an increasing demand for rural and scenic land, just to allow town-dwellers to live a satisfactory life.

The misuse of our environment is a major problem of the British environment. As in all highly developed industrial economies the

---

[1] Conservation Society, 'Britain's Population Problem'.
[2] Brian McConnell, *Britain in the Year 2000*.

waste products of the consumer society cause environmental problems. The growth of disposable cans and bottles make a litter that ruins our scenic countryside. Such disposable trash constitutes the wastes of the consumer society, which left unremedied will cause a major, and perhaps permanent eyesore.

Industrial derelict land is another major problem in an economy concentrating on producing maximum returns. The official estimate of derelict land is 100,000 acres, but the real figure is likely to be somewhere near 250,000 acres. The difference occurs because the Government does not include spoil-heaps that are in use; the Aberfan slagheap, which killed 144 children in 1966 was not considered derelict under the present tests of measurement. This figure is being added to each year by a net figure of 3,500 acres, since according to the Civic Trust, schemes of reclamation do not keep pace with the increasing output of waste from the extractive industries; mining coal, sand and gravel, china clay, gypsum and brick clay.[1]

Pollution of our environment is a major problem. Sir Frank Fraser Darling, as part of his Reith Lectures in 1969 calls population and pollution 'the two great problems of our age, and pollution is a function of population increase'. Pollution exists in the sea, in the air and in our rivers and fields. It is all around us.

Smoke is the obvious air pollutant; each year Britain produces one million tons of smoke. A smoke-produced smog in 1952 prematurely killed 4,000 bronchial cripples in London, and as a result action in the shape of the Clean Air Acts was taken. When a similar smog hit London ten years later, the death rate was only 700. Dr. R. S. Craxford, who runs the National Air Pollutant Survey estimates that 'Industrial smoke has well-nigh disappeared. The amounts of smoke are now only one third of what they used to be, and one quarter of what they used to be in London'.

Nevertheless Brian McConnell is able to assert that 'Britain has the foulest air in Europe. Deaths due to bronchitis in Britain are 28,257 compared with Germany's 10,111, France's 2,606 and Holland's 1,768'. Obvious allowance must be made for the damper climate of Britain but the varying rates of bronchial deaths still match closely the national distribution of smoke.[2]

Although the Clean Air Acts control the output of smoke, they do not contain the other pollutants contained in the air we breathe, such

---

[1] John Barr, *The Environmental Handbook*, pp. 132.

[2] Brian McConnell, *Britain in the Year 2000*.

as sulphur dioxide, carbon monoxide, fluoride, asbestos fumes and lead poisoning.

The annual output of sulphur dioxide is six million tons, most of which falls back onto the ground as sulphuric acid which eats into materials, buildings and cars, and can cause illness and death to human beings. Although not as dangerous as smog it is the next most dangerous pollutant of our atmosphere. Perhaps the worst indictment of our cost-conscious society is that the sulphur content of the atmosphere could be reduced to a fraction by planned heating arrangements using many more central boilers on housing estates, such as that being incorporated in the new GLC estate at Kidbrooke SE9 and in apartment blocks like those built in the new town of Washington, County Durham.

Carbon monoxide from car exhausts is the next biggest nuisance and is highly dangerous. Reference has already been made to the dangerous levels during the rush hour in Oxford Street. Research into the effects of carbon monoxide poisoning has been carried out by the Brighton College of Technology and by Mr. John Lewis of *Which*. They found that, although the long term health risk is not a direct danger, exposure to the poisonous gases does affect performance.

Lead poisoning is another major problem. Output in Britain is estimated to be around 10,000 tons a year from car exhausts alone. Lead poisoning of water and food is a related problem. In 1963 the World Health Organization recommended a limit of 0·05 milligrammes of lead per litre of drinking water from the tap. A. J. Tolley of Liverpool University found that in samples of water from Britain's towns, nine of them exceeded the limit, and, after the WHO had doubled the limit in 1970, three still, exceeded this increased limit.

By comparison, asbestos and fluoride poisoning are minor with only localized effect, but anyone who has travelled past a brickworks can testify to the environmental effects resulting from the production of bricks. In addition to the above mentioned poisonous pollutants we dump approximately 8½ million tons of waste into the air each year. In areas of high industrial activity such as Billingham on Teeside, or the Black Country in Staffordshire this output falls back at the rate of 1,000 tons per square mile per year.

After air, rivers are the biggest pollution danger. Most of our sewage, and much rubbish that is too wet to burn, is deposited in the rivers of our country. Rivers, that half a century ago would have brought a gleam to the eyes of Isaac Walton, now run dead, not a living thing being able to breathe within their waters. Because our laws controlling effluent standards are fifty years old, industrial wastes are allowed to overpower the bacteria in the rivers, use up the oxygen and turn the rivers into cesspools. Britain has 20,000 miles of rivers and one in every four is polluted; one in twenty is so contaminated that it scarcely warrrants the word river.

Pollution occurs in our fields too. Pesticides like DDT, compounds containing mercury and other nitrates build up and cause major problems. At sea the Torrey Canyon disaster in 1966 served to highlight a problem that has existed through polychlorinated biphenyls and radioactive material for a long period of time.

Urban growth and the quality of life

In America, the proportion of the population living in an urban environment is 67 per cent: in Britain the proportion is 82 per cent. Urban communities are the norm and if we are to lead satisfactory lives within them, we must understand the concept fully and the consequences of living crowded together into small areas.

One obvious constraint of urban living is the lack of privacy. The Londoners who demonstrated against the intrusion of the new overhead motorway, Westway, into their lives because they lived alongside the viaduct made a very important point. Even if you succeed in getting away from your fellow human beings, it is very difficult to get away from the physical environment, or from the noise it makes. You do not have to live near airports to hear the sonic booms that Concorde will make or to be aware of the perpetual noise of traffic.

Personal freedom will also be constrained. It is impossible to live in a densely populated area, where demand for resources will outstrip supply, without being subject to rationing of some kind. The price you have to pay is 'No Parking' signs, and 'No Entry' signs.

All constraints to personal freedom and intrusion into privacy set up frustrations that cause stress and psychological damage. We have already talked about the effects of overcrowding in animals. But these stresses apply to human beings no less for they too are part of the animal kingdom and are subject to the laws of the animal world. To crowd large numbers of human beings into smaller areas as the density of population increases has led to the acceptance of 'high-rise living' as a way of life for many thousands, who, if they had a choice, would still choose the traditional two storey building with private garden. And studies have shown that cities receive 15 per cent less sunshine on horizontal surfaces and 10 per cent more rainfall. Cloudy days are more frequent and there is 30 per cent more fog in summer and 100 per cent more fog in winter. The incidence of many diseases is higher. Crime and mental sickness rates are higher. Without taking an alarmist view, all these potential hazards must be considered in the context of population size.

CHAPTER 7
STUDIES IN POPULATION POLICY

In the foregoing chapters, the history of population growth in Britain has been examined, against the background of the growth of world population, the various theories of population, and the concepts that are used in a study of demography. This last chapter looks at possible population policies that can be adopted to solve different population problems.[1]

The growth of world population
The world population is near 3,160 million. The growth rate is 2 per cent per annum, which means that an additional 65 million people come to live in the world each year. At the present rate of growth, the population of the world will be over 4 billion by 1975 and will reach 7·5 billions by the end of the century. World population will double every 35 years, which is near enough to the Malthusian geometrical progression figure of doubling every generation to cause grave concern.

Put another way, the equivalent population to that of a country appreciably larger than the United Kingdom, comes into being each year, and a child born today would see the population of the world quadruple in his lifetime at this rate.

The total growth of world population, and continental growth rates are illustrated by the diagrams below.

The population problem is one of size – of aggregate demand and aggregate supply. We have seen that the rate of growth of world population is increasing at a fast pace. The inference is that unless world food supply increases at the same rate there will be famine on a world scale. Food supply must increase faster than population increase if all men and women are to be well-fed with balanced diets, for at this moment a large percentage of the world's population are suffering from malnutrition.

In the last ten or fifteen years food supplies have increased faster than population increase. The figures quoted from the *Barclays Bank*

---

[1] One very good case study is the study of Mauritius contained in *Case Studies in Economics*, ed. C. D. Sandford (Macmillan).

THE POPULATION TREE

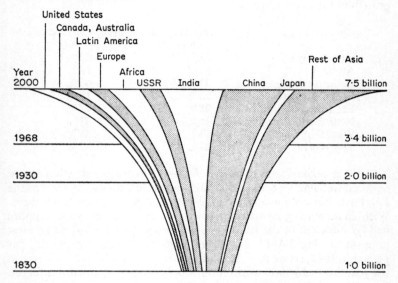

Fig. 34

Source: *Economist*, May 8, 1965 and December 20, 1969

On the most likely assumptions made by the United Nations' forecasters, world population will reach 4.3 billion by 1980, 6.0 billion by the turn of the century. Europe's share of the total will fall from 14.2% in 1960 to 11.2% by 1980 and 8.8% by 2000; North America's share from 6.7% to 6.1% to 5.9%. by the 1980s, Europeans will be outnumbered by Africans; by the 1999s by Latin Americans also.

| | Population (in millions) | | Average annual increase 1960–1980 | |
	1964	1980	%	millions
China	690	840	1·3	8·5
India	467	662	2·1	9·1
Japan	97	111	0·9	0·8
USSR	229	278	1·4	3·0
USA	192	241	1·4	2·5
EEC	177	193	0·6	1·0
EFTA	92	98	0·5	0·4
of which				
Britain	54	57	0·3	0·2

Review, 1967 (August), gives some idea of the relationship between growth of the two variables.

Country	% growth of population	% growth of food supply (1952/3–1964/5)
East Europe	18%	62%
Africa	36%	32%
Latin America	37%	40%
North America	23%	19%
Far East	28%	42%
Near East	36%	41%
West Europe	11%	35%
The World	27%	37%

So the problem is not so much a failure of aggregate size, but one of regional imbalance; today over half the world population lives in the Far East, but only a quarter of the food supply comes from there. With an increasing growth rate the problem of whether food supplies will be sufficient in the future is obviously a question of the greatest importance. The FAO has made a target of 2,400 calories per day per person in 1962, rising to 2,560 calories in 1975 and 2,620 calories in the year 2,000. In 1962 world food supply exactly equalled this target. By the year 2,000, if the target is to be met, an increase of 12 per cent in population will mean an increase in food supply in the order of 175 per cent.

There seems to be no real reason for worry on this score. Colin Clark, in his book *Population Growth and Land Use*, has estimated that the world land area is capable of supporting a population of twenty-eight billions, 'or ten times its population. This leaves us a very ample margin for land which we wish to set aside for recreation or other purposes.' This estimate is based on the hypothesis that today the world feeds off only 3·4 billion acres, which if land was used sensibly and extensively, could be stretched to 13–17 billion.[1] At present Africa has only 30 per cent of her land area under cultivation, China 29 per cent, Latin America 25 per cent and the USSR only 27 per cent. With Australia only half under cultivation, there is ample room for expansion. Dramatic innovations in fertilizers, food strains and synthetic foods could increase food supply tremendously in a short period of time.

These global problems are much more intense in certain regions. In

[1] *Economist*, December 20, 1969.

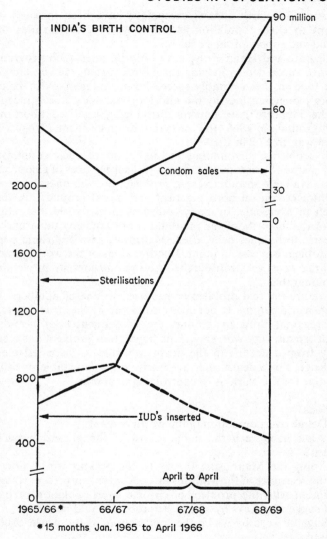

Fig. 35. *India's Birth Control – 1965/66 – 1968/69*
(*Economist*, December 10, 1969)

117

India, massive birth control campaigns have been initiated in an attempt to curb population growth. Fig. 35 gives an idea of the demand and supply of the problem.

Singapore and Hong Kong have both initiated such programmes and have succeeded in halving their birth rate in the last ten years. Japan too, has been notably successful in this field. With Japanese doctors pioneering the rhythm and loop methods of contraception, and the Japanese governments introducing legalized abortion on health grounds in 1948, the birth rate dropped from 23.7 just after the last war, to 17·2 in 1960.

The problems surrounding the initiation of such country-wide family planning programmes are not just simply ones of resources. As always, available resources are a problem, but the questions roused by contraception on both practical and moral grounds are just as difficult to overcome. In many countries in the world, the religious faith of the majority of the inhabitants prevents any unnatural contraceptive techniques being used. Mauritius, with a chronic population problem is a case in point. In other areas of the world, practical difficulties of travel, transport, education and literacy prove almost insurmountable.

Therefore the real problem comes back to one of numbers. Even though world famine is not likely to occur in the near future, the great regional imbalances, and the consequences of population growth remain very worrying. This population problem has resulted largely from a decline in the death rate due to increased medical knowledge. Since death rates are likely to remain stable or fall, the only hope for the world is to control the birth rate.

Questions

1. Define overpopulation in the world context.

2. What have been the main causes of the present population problem?

3. Apply the Malthusian theory to the present world situation. State the relevance of the Malthusian concept to our present situation.

4. Faced with the problem of chronic overpopulation prepare a report suggesting ways by which the problem could be solved.

5. Suggest ways by which the food supply of the world could be increased.

An optimum population for Britain?

On May 17, 1971, a Select Committee of the House of Commons

reported that the pressure of population growth in Britain could make everyday life 'intolerable'. The Chairman of the Select Committee, Mr. Airey Neave, MP, declined to determine an optimum population; he preferred to talk in terms of 'publicizing the effects of population levels and their consequences, the role of family limitation and socially responsible parenthood'. But, if one is going to talk about everyday life becoming intolerable, then one must have some concept of the optimum population.

The concept of 'optimum' population is difficult. The optimum position depends on so many factors, principally the state of technical knowledge and the output, in terms of total production of goods and services and need-satisfaction, of the economy. Therefore much that is said about optimum population is subjective, reflecting the economist's personal viewpoint of the chosen benefits from the economy relative to the level of population. Keynes asked, 'Is not a country overpopulated when its standards are lower than they would be if its numbers were less?' Even this is subjective for much depends on the meaning of standards.

One way to analyse the problem is to imagine Britain with a population appreciably higher than our present fifty-eight millions, and then to postulate the effects of this level of population.

If population were increased to 1,000 million, a figure that is nearly twenty times our present level of population, there would be both advantages and disadvantages. The major population effect would be that we would have a very high density, but this density would produce beneficial effects, which are important to take account of. Because of the economies of large scale production, the cost per head of public utilities such as electricity and gas, tele-communications and public transport would decrease, giving cheaper prices and greater efficiency. Technology in all fields would make tremendous strides; the mass production of synthetic foods would be possible; large scale improvements in public transport would increase, as demand increased and private transport became impossible; whole city areas might be able to be roofed in, affording continuous protection against inclement weather and good sports facilities; massive increments of automation and capital investment would concentrate industry into capital-dominated industries, thus leaving more time for leisure and recreational pursuits; whole ranges of artistic and indoor facilities and pursuits would benefit from this increased interest and demand; new living styles and architecture could be introduced; intellectual life might be stimulated, since one could expect several Newtons,

119

Shakespeares, Jane Austens and Constables to be alive at the same time.[1]

Against these advantages, there would be several disadvantages. Technical problems would loom large. Food distribution, sewage disposal, pollution problems, important now, would increase. Human problems would be even more important; there would be fewer open spaces; the sheer pressure of people might become such a strain that psychological disorders could become a major killer; open air and open spaces would become a rarity; natural foods and materials would be practically unknown.

At a lower level of population, say thirty millions, there would be advantages and disadvantages too. A lower population level would decrease the average density of population; if the decrease took place in the highly populated areas of the country – the South and Midlands – the chronic housing shortage which exists at present, would disappear. In housing areas, there would be more space available for gardens, the number of high-rise dwellings, which have caused great social problems, would disappear, because they would no longer be needed. Britain would return to a duplex living style. School classes would decrease in size. The demand for food production would drop meaning that most, if not all the demand for staple food could be satisfied by domestic production. The pressure on roads and other amenities would decrease with proportional advantages for the whole of the population, and open spaces and coastal areas would be free from the human litter and pollution that threatens their existence now.

Against these obvious advantages are worrying disadvantages that make critics of our present level of population seem naive in their aggressive attacks on population growth. The economic problems created would be very great. There are still economists who believe that this country is short of labour. One reason why Britain has done so badly in the economic growth stakes since the war is that its work force has grown very slowly compared with other countries. If this is so, then a decrease in labour supply will create untold problems. The age distribution of the country would edge upwards, so that the old became a larger part of the total than the young. This would mean that the younger, working population, would have to work proportionately harder if they were to continue to support the bigger burden

---

[1] J. H. Fremlin, 'An Optimum Population for Britain', *New Scientist*, December 21, 1967.

of the non-working population. In international trade we would be setting ourselves at a disadvantage, competing against countries with a denser population and a larger home market, from which to develop. One of the most cogent arguments for Britain's entry into the Common Market is just this importance gained from a bigger home market. To decrease the size of the home market would be to deny benefits which we seek at present, and which some countries, in particular the United States, have found to their advantage.

It is possible to imagine policies to achieve either of these levels. There is a third possibility, that of effecting a stabilization policy. The mechanics of such a policy are firstly an awareness of the right level of population consistent with some concept of the 'optimum' population, secondly the ability to calculate a replacement rate, at which the present level of population is stabilized so that as members die they are replaced by newcomers, and thirdly, the sheer mechanics of effecting population control, in a country with wide differences of social, religious, moral and ethnic backgrounds.

There are many experts who argue that Britain's present population level is around the optimum point and that the government should take active steps to hold it at about 58–63 millions.

To achieve this, a replacement rate of 2·2 children per family would have to be achieved, this being consistent with a birth rate of around 14·0. This would give zero rate of growth.

This zero rate of increase needs a positive policy to enable it to be achieved. At present the average family size is around 2·4 children per family, and recent statistics suggest that in marriages where the age of the bride is twenty or under, the average family size will be as high as 2·8 children. The population would first need to be fully in possession of the means to control family size and secondly it would need to be induced to limit family size to the national target.

The first would require a comprehensive family planning service, perhaps on the National Health Service, being given to *all* members of the population who need it, whether married or unmarried. The need for contraceptives comes from both married and unmarried persons and is often not bounded by the 'norms' of sexual behaviour put out by society. Thus, teenagers are as much in need of contraceptive advice as men and women in their twenties and thirties, and often men and women in their twenties and thirties need re-educating in the necessities of family planning.

This need can only be satisfied if there is a nationwide network of family planning clinics and a comprehensive distribution system for contraceptives of all types. In April 1968 the FPA criticized the local health authorities for their slow progress towards providing such a service. Legislation passed in the Family Planning Act 1967 laid down machinery for a full family planning service, but a year later only forty-nine out of a total of 104 local authorities were providing such a service. 'One in six local authorities provided a full service.' (FPA.)

Much has been written about the distribution of contraceptive devices in under-developed countries with chronic overpopulation problems, but little has been said about the difficulties of obtaining essential supplies in developed nations. W. Thompson and D. T. Lewis, in their book *Population Problems* list six requirements for effective birth control campaigns. These are (*a*) cheap contraceptives, (*b*) effective contraception, (*c*) devices which are easy to understand and apply, (*d*) devices with no side effects, (*e*) devices which are usable under primitive conditions, (*f*) devices which conflict as little as possible with the religious beliefs of the population and the traditional reproductive practices. The obtaining of the devices is not considered an important requirement, for in a well-ordered campaign it is assumed that this will have been dealt with. Yet, in a developed country like Britain it is just this simple requirement that is often missing. Many are the possibilities of unwanted pregnancy because contraceptives are not available when the need for them arises, a factor which must affect our problem of unwanted children.

In Britain, even if we solve the problem of not producing unwanted babies, this would only relieve the position of perhaps 200,000 – 300,000 births per year. It would be a start, but it would not, by itself, solve the problem and stabilize population growth. Other problems remain.

A large number of women have an emotional and sub-conscious drive to become pregnant, even though they are unmarried. Sometimes it is fear, sometimes a drive to fulfil themselves as females, sometimes it is a trap set for marriage, sometimes it is a feeling of loneliness, sometimes it is just unsympathetic handling or bad family planning advice. Whatever the reason this group of women represent a sizeable problem. The FPA estimate that 6 per cent of their clinic population fail to return for further advice; surveys show that 30–50 per cent of married women have unwanted pregnancies; 23 per cent of all families with more than six children have resources below the minimum Ministry of Social Security level to support them.

Even these problems are minor compared to the social and religious problems involved in a comprehensive population control policy. To achieve this, the concept that men and women have a right – a natural right – to have as many children as they wish will have to be influenced: the number of *wanted* children would have to be reduced and this involves a number of social and religious problems.

In a democratic society a comprehensive population policy will have to be voluntary if it is to succeed within the tenets of society. The Select Committee have already dismissed the idea that couples might be forced into family limitation; it is unlikely that any British Government within the foreseeable future will resort to such measures as 'fertility control agents introduced into the water supply' or marketable licences to have children, or temporary sterilization of girls via time capsules, or any such *Brave New World* concepts, which have from time to time been suggested by population economists. It is possible that in time the government might move in the direction of inducements for men and women to have smaller families such as reduction of family allowances or tax penalties for parents of more than two children. Possible also would be financial inducements for later marriage: grants for first marriages when both partners are over a certain age. Such measures have been tried before in certain countries and have often failed. In Switzerland, during the nineteenth century legislation to encourage later marriage was nullified by a large increase in illegitimacy.

In our present age, when marriage is no longer the price men have to pay for sexual relationships, and sex is not the price women have to pay for marriages, a more positive approach is necessary. People will have to be informed of the dangers of excessive population growth. The key figures in this are women, and in particular the young woman. She must be given an alternative to child-bearing which is satisfying for her. As Gerald Leach has observed, 'we need a different life style; better opportunities of higher education for women, leading to more satisfying jobs as an alternative to having babies in the earlier rather than the later twenties.'

Questions

1. What is meant by 'optimum population?' What factors must be taken into account in deciding the optimum population of a country?

2. Would you describe Britain as being overpopulated at the

present time? Consider the economic and social costs and benefits of high and low density population.

3. What problems exist in trying to initiate a population policy in Britain?

4. What methods can you think of to stabilize Britain's population?

5. What is the nature of Britain's population problem? Is it the absolute size of population, the rate of growth or the composition of our population that is worrying?

QUESTIONS

1. Examine the economic effects on both countries of the migration of labour to Great Britain from an under-developed Commonwealth country.

2. What are the causes and consequences of the 'Drift to the South' in Great Britain? What economic measures might be used to control this movement?

3. 'The size of the population in the United Kingdom is less important than its age structure and geographical distribution.' Comment.

4. Why is it that some countries are concerned because population is growing too slowly, while others fear too rapid an increase?

5. Examine the possible economic consequences of changes in (a) the size, and (b) the age structure of a country's population.

6. Explain what is meant by 'the working population'. What factors affects its size?

7. What is meant by the 'brain drain' and how might it be stopped?

8. Examine the economic effects on a country of large scale emigration of young working people without dependants.

9. Discuss the economic problems arising from urban concentration of the population.

10. Examine the effects of large scale immigration to the United Kingdom.

11. What factors are responsible for recent changes in the United Kingdom population?

12. What would be the economic effects of an increasing rate of growth of population?

13. For every extra mouth to feed there is soon an extra pair of hands to work, therefore the population of a country can never be too big. Discuss this proposition with particular reference to your own country.

14. What is meant by 'the danger of overpopulation'? Discuss its relevance to the present time.

15. Consider the economic effects of a large increase in emigration from the UK.

16. What is meant by overpopulation?

17. What changes can be expected in the British population during the next twenty years? Discuss the economic consequences of these changes.

READING LIST

Textbooks

I. Bowen, *Population* (Nisbet)
Robinson, *Population* (Key Discussion Book)
Royal Commission on Population, HMSO. Cmnd. 7695
P. K. Kelsall, *Population* (Longmans)
J. R. Hicks, *The Social Framework* (OUP)
Malthus, *Treatise on Population*
D. V. Glass, *The Struggle for Population* (Oxford)
C. Cippolla, *Economic History of World Population* (Penguin)
P. Deane, *The First Industrial Revolution*
J. Hubback, *The Population of Britain* (Penguin)
Giles, *Understanding Economics* (Ginn)
H. W. Flinn, *British Population Growth* (Macmillan)
Johns, *The Social Structure of Britain* (Pergamon)
C. Park, *Population Explosion* (Heinemann)

General Readers

G. R. Taylor, *The Domesday Book* (Thames and Hudson)
Peterson, *The Politics of Population* (Gollancz)
G. M. Carstairs, *This Island Now* (Penguin)
R. Fletcher, *The Family and Marriage* (Penguin)
A. Allison (ed.), *Population Control* (Penguin)
B. McConnell, *Britain in the Year 2000* (NEL)
P. Ehrlich, *The Population Bomb* (Ballantine Books)
Fraser Darling, *Wilderness and Plenty* (OUP)
John Barr, *The Environmental Handbook* (Ballantine Books)
K. Jones and A. D. Smith, *The Economic Impact of Commonwealth Immigration* (CUP)

Articles

Grant, 'A Demographic Approach to Social and Economic History', *Economics*, Spring 1965
Liversedge, 'The English Population of the 18th and 19th Centuries', *Economics*, Autumn 196?
Hawkes, 'The Air We Breathe', *Telegraph Magazine*, May 28, 1971
Hawkes, 'Who Are The British?', *Observer*, February 12 and 19, 1967
'Britain's Population Problem', Conservation Society 1971

'Why Britain needs a Population Policy', Conservation Society 1971

'Too many or too few', *Economist*, April 5, 1969

'Pressure of Population', *London and Cambridge Economic Review*, December 1964

Parry Lewis, 'Young People and the Pattern of the Economy' *Lloyds Bank Review*, July 1961

E. J. Mishan, 'Immigration; long run economic effects', *Lloyds Bank Review*, November 1967

Mishan and L. Needleman, 'Immigration; some economic effects', *Lloyds Bank Review*, July 1966

David Eversley, '*The Population Explosion*', Purnell's History of the 20th Century

INDEX

INDEX